I dedicate this book to my father, Daniel J. McCabe.
Thanks for supporting my dreams and encouraging me in
my academic pursuits.

In memory of my aunt who died so that others may live.

Contents

Contents   vii

List of Tables

Preface

It all happened one day when my eyes fell across a page revealing a hidden secret from ages past: the Isis cult. My heart was instantly ignited with a passion that gripped me and propelled me to research like never before. Could this be the answer that I was looking for? Or the untapped revelation that might bring women equality in the body of Christ? Little did I know that the next few years of my life would become a relentless pursuit to uncover all available material on this historical background. While this work originally started as a historical analysis of 1 Peter 3.1, it soon took on a life of its own and found its resting place in the vicinity of Ephesus. Ephesus was home of many pagan religions, one of which was the Isis cult.

This work will trace the steps necessary for intersection with the biblical text, commencing with Isis and her birthplace in Egypt and concluding with Isis as a possible historical background behind 1 Timothy 2.12-14. The goal of this investigation is to discover the potential of the Isis cult for biblical studies by releasing it from the rigors of archaeology and tentatively intersecting it with the biblical text. What implications the Isis cult has for the future of biblical studies is yet unknown, but this work will illuminate this historical reality of antiquity.

Elizabeth A. McCabe
Cincinnati, OH
August 23, 2005

Acknowledgments

First and foremost, all praise and honor go to the Lord Jesus Christ who made this work a reality. I praise You, Lord, for leading me to the idea of the Isis cult and entrusting me with such a task. I thank You for the motivation, determination, passion, and strength You have given me through the years of research. You truly are the author of this work and You have brought it to completion. You deserve all glory for whatever this work may accomplish. Thanks also to those who have faithfully prayed for me and this work over the years.

Second, I want to thank all who have been instrumental in the writing and research process. Much thanks goes to Dr. William Baker who has been an invaluable source of help and assistance in this process. Your expertise has been much appreciated, and I am blessed to have had the privilege of working with you. Thanks also to the library staff at Cincinnati Christian University who have been most accommodating during this time. And many thanks is due to the faculty and staff at Cincinnati Christian University. Your feedback, criticism, and assistance have been most helpful. This work would not have been the same without your input.

Appreciation also goes to my family who have acted as συνεργοί, in the production of this work. They have watched me labor over this work for a few years. I greatly thank you for your patience in this time of research and writing. A very special thanks to Barbara McCabe for proofreading without complaint, Kimberley Ernstes for her constant source of encouragement, Timothy Ernstes for technical support, Matt McCabe for the use of his computer, and to all others who have helped keep my dreams alive. Without your help, this work would not be possible.

Abbreviations

AAWW	Anzeiger der Österreichischen Akademie der Wissenschaften
'Abod. Zar	*'Abodah Zarah*
AJA	*American Journal of Archaeology*
ANET	*Ancient Near Eastern Texts Relating to the Old Testament*
ANRW	*Aufstieg und Niedergang der römischen Welt: Geschichte und Kultur Roms im Spiegel der neueren Forschung.* Edited by H. Temporini and W. Haase. Berlin, 1972-
Ant.	*Antonius*
Apol.	*Apologia*
Apul.	Apuleius
ASV	American Standard Version
Aug.	*Divus Augustus*
BDB	Brown, F., S. R. Driver, and C. A. Briggs. *A Hebrew and English Lexicon of the Old Testament.*
BCH	*Bulletin de correspondance hellénique*
BDAG	Danker, F. W., W. Bauer, W. F. Arndt, and F. W. Gingrich. *Greek-English Lexicon of the New Testament and Other Early Christian Literature.* 3d ed. Chicago, 2000.
CBQ	*Catholic Biblical Quarterly*
DAE	*Dictionary of Ancient Egypt*
Dig.	*Digesta*
DLNT	*Dictionary of the Later New Testament and Its Developments.* Edited by R. P. Martin and P. H. Davids. Downers Grove, 1997.
DPL	*Dictionary of Paul and His Letters.* Edited by G. F. Hawthorne and R. P. Martin. Downers Grove, 1993.

De Is. et Os.	*De Iside et Osiride*
Diod. Sic.	Diodorus Siculus
EPRO	Etudes préliminaires aux religions orientales dans l'empire romain
ERE	*Encyclopaedia of Religion and Ethics.* Edited by J. Hastings. 13 vols. New York. 1908-27. Reprint, 7 vols., 1951.
Firm. Mat.	Firmicus Maternus
FRA	*Fontes Historiae Religionis Aegyptiacae.* Edited by Hopfner. 1922.
Gell.	Aulus Gellius
HTS	Harvard Theological Studies
JÖAI	Jahreshefte des Österreichischen archäologischen Instituts
JSNT	*Journal for the Study of the New Testament*
LCL	Loeb Classical Library
LXX	Septuagint
Macrob.	Macrobius
Metam.	*Metamorphoses*
MMM	*Man, Myth, and Magic: The Illustrated Encyclopedia of Myth, Religion, and the Unknown.* Edited by Richard Cavendish. 12 vols. New York: Marshall Cavendish, 1985.
NA	*Noctes Atticae*
NASB	New American Standard Bible
NIV	New International Version
NKJV	New King James Version
NIBCNT	New International Biblical Commentary on the New Testament
NICNT	New International Commentary on the New Testament
OCD	*Oxford Classical Dictionary.* Edited by S. Hornblower and A. Spawforth. 3d ed. Oxford, 1999.
Od.	*Odyssey*
P. Oxy.	*Papyrus Oxyrhynchus*
Plut.	Plutarch
Pyr.	*Pyramid Texts*
RMA	*Roman und Mysterium in der Antike* by R. Merkelbach. Berlin, 1962.
Rom. Ant.	*Roman Antiquities*
Sat.	*Saturnalia*
SIRIS	*Sylloge inscriptionum religionis Isiacae et Sarapiacae* by L. Vidman. Religionsgeschichtliche Versuche und Vorarbeiten 28. Berlin, 1969.

Suet.	Suetonius
TDNT	*Theological Dictionary of the New Testament.* Edited by G. Kittel and G. Friedrich. Translated by G. W. Bromiley. 10 vols. Grand Rapids, 1964-76.
Tert.	Tertullian
WBC	Word Biblical Commentary

Introduction

This work provides an examination of the Isis cult with preliminary exploration into New Testament studies. The purpose of this investigation is to determine the extent of the intersection between the Isis cult and the biblical text. Specific attention will be given to Isis as an historical context to 1 Timothy, particularly how the Legend of Ra and Isis could link with 1 Tim 2.12-14 by reinforcing the validity of the creation story. To accomplish this study, Isis will be examined in her initial birthplace (Egypt), followed by her infiltration into Greco-Roman society, and finally as a possible historical background for 1 Timothy. A brief history of the Isis cult will suffice to provide a historical basis for this investigation.

The origin of Isis will first be described. Attention will be given to the nine gods and goddesses of the Heliopolis (or the Ennead). According to Egyptian mythology, Isis and Osiris are two of these pagan deities. Isis becomes enamored with her brother (Osiris) and she marries him. This pagan myth makes inroads into Egyptian society, for Egyptian men are allowed to marry their sisters because of the successful marriage of Isis to her brother.[1] While Osiris is also king, his reign is short-lived since he is murdered by his crafty brother Set (or Typhon). Isis saves the day by taking the throne and reigning over the land. Isis sets such a notable example that it is ordained that "the queen should have greater power and honour than the king."[2]

The example of Isis makes its imprint upon Egyptian society, especially in the reign of Cleopatra. Cleopatra is recognized as the "new Isis" according to Plutarch[3] and makes efforts to associate herself with this pagan goddess. Her husband, Antony, is portrayed as Osiris and is criticized for allowing his wife to have the upper hand in the relationship. Cleopatra exerts her power over her husband in terms of decisions during her reign.[4] Egyptian society is also affected by the Isis cult in marital relationships, according to Diodorus

1

Siculus. Diodorus writes, "Among private persons the wife should enjoy authority over her husband, the husbands agreeing in the marriage contract that they will be obedient in all things to their wives."[5]

Isis is portrayed as a model for Egyptian women and is believed to be the foundation for outstanding women in Egypt.[6] Isis is believed to be responsible for making the power of women equal to that of men as evident from *Papyrus Oxyrhynchus XI.1380*.[7] The personification of Isis, Cleopatra, also portrays herself equal to a man as demonstrated in her reign. Isis is also believed to be responsible in protecting her husband Osiris,[8] and the one who devised marriage contracts as evident in the Kyme Aretalogy.[9]

However, Isis is recognized beyond her status for the emancipation of women and also is thought to hold the power of salvation in her hands. S. Young comments that the account of Isis as told by Plutarch (one of the primary sources for Isiac study) entails "powerful salvation imagery in which Isis not only cares for the dead but gives them new life."[10] Isis is described as a "savior goddess" and "will care for and restore to life all of her devotees."[11] Isis also holds rewards for her faithful initiates and is believed to bestow salvation upon those who are devoted to her.[12]

Employing the historical-critical method, this work will begin by analyzing the origin and institutionalizing of the Isis cult. The first chapter will discuss the basic myth of Isis and the effects of Isis in Egyptian history. Cleopatra will be given special attention as the living embodiment of Isis as well the Ptolemaic dynasty being instrumental in the promotion of this pagan goddess. This will be followed by a discussion of Isis in the Greco-Roman world in chapter two. The cult of Isis overflowed into the Greco-Roman world and can be placed in the context of Greco-Roman society due to the archaeological evidence for the Isis cult in the Greco-Roman empire.[13] However, the Isis cult is not the only religion in practice during this time but comes into being during a syncretistic age. The gradual shift of sensitivity in religions, such as decreased satisfaction with institutionalized state religions, makes the Isis cult a much more attractive religion since it is a personalized belief system.

The Isis cult gains a permanent foothold in Rome and prevails in the midst of persecution. While the Isis cult is originally met with opposition, later emperors accept and approve of the Isis cult.[14] Rome sets an example for the rest of the provinces through building the Isis Campense in the Campus Martius which is "the greatest of the Roman Iseums."[15] The Isis cult serves as a link between the two otherwise isolated entities and helps to bridge the provinces and Rome together into a unified whole.

Chapter three will discuss the relevance of Isis to New Testament studies. This chapter will demonstrate that the Isis cult provides a suitable backdrop for New Testament study. The archaeological evidence from the Isis cult helps to bolster this line of thought. Isiac evidence preexisted that of Christianity in many cases and is evident in the cities that Paul visited on his missionary journeys. This is not to ignore other religions in the New Testament era, for in this syncretistic age a number of religions hold considerable appeal. The Isis cult is one of the mystery religions which comes into popularity "in an era of individualism, when men were no longer looking to religion for guaranties of a racial or national order."[16] People can also relate to Isis as a benevolent goddess who promises to give her devotees eternal life and help them with their woes in life in stark contrast to the impersonal Roman state religion designed to usher in peace and prosperity for the Roman government. This chapter will also investigate Isiac beliefs and practices comparable to Paul's teachings. These include Isis as a savior goddess, baptism in the Isis cult, archaeological evidence for water facilities in Iseums, and a discussion of resurrection.

Chapter four will continue this discussion by examining concepts of freedom, salvation, resurrection, and baptism in Pauline Christianity. These concepts will be explored with the help of Pauline scholars, such as J. Dunn. This approach will be enhanced by employing a statistical analysis of the frequency of how Paul uses certain words, such as ἐλευθερία, ἐλεύθερος, and ἐλευθερόω. Because of this similarity between the Isis cult and Pauline Christianity, these two religions may have been appealing to a great number of people, drawing from the same people predisposed to these ideas. Contrasts between the Isis cult and Pauline Christianity will also be noted here.

The comparisons and contrasts with Pauline Christianity will be concluded with Isis as a possible context for 1 Timothy. Chapter five will focus on the pagan religious environment in order to demonstrate that the Isis cult is a possible background for 1 Timothy. Archaeological, epigraphical, numismatic, and literary evidence for the Isis cult will be presented for Ephesus. A closer look at the contents of 1 Timothy in view of the Isis cult will also be provided here. Concerning the Isis cult, the Legend of Ra and Isis will be discussed from the standpoint of 1 Tim 2.12-14. The conclusion will retrace the steps developed throughout the work as well as affirming the implications that the Isis cult may hold for New Testament studies and suggest avenues for further study.

NOTES

1. Diod. Sic., *Library of History* 1.27.1.
2. Diod. Sic., *Library of History* 1.27.2 (Oldfather, LCL).
3. Plut., *Ant.* 54.6 (B. Perrin, LCL).
4. F. Hooper, *Roman Realities* (Detroit: Wayne University Press, 1979), 306.
5. Diod. Sic., *Library of History* 1.27.2 (Oldfather, LCL).

6. D. B. Nagle, *The Ancient World: A Social and Cultural History*, 5th ed. (New Jersey: Prentice Hall, 2002), 51. One such outstanding woman in Egyptian society is undoubtedly Cleopatra.

7. *P. Oxy. XI.1380* is a well-recognized archaeological document, dating from the early second century AD, providing various titles for Isis. This text is provided in *Maenads, Martyrs, Matrons, Monastics: A Sourcebook on Women's Religions in the Greco-Roman World*, R. S. Kraemer, ed. (Philadelphia: Fortress Press, 1988), 367-68. (Hereafter, only the notation *P. Oxy. XI.1380* will be referenced.)

8. See M. Lichtheim, *The New Kingdom*, vol. 2 of *Ancient Egyptian Literature* (Berkley: University of California Press, 1976), 83, for the complete inscription, dating from BC 1567-1320.

9. The Kyme Aretalogy is a first-person account of the works of Isis, also known as the "Praises of Isis" (F. C. Grant, ed., *Hellenistic Religions: The Age of Syncretism*; New York: Liberal Arts Press, 1953, 131). This work was discovered in Kyme (or Cyme) in Asia Minor and is a recension attributed to the second or third century AD. The Kyme Aretalogy is "probably a Hellenistic revision of an Egyptian hymn extolling the goddess" (Kraemer, *Sourcebook on Women's Religions*, 411). The complete text of the Kyme Aretalogy is provided by Kraemer, *Sourcebook on Women's Religions*, 367-70. (Hereafter, only the notation, "the Kyme Aretalogy," will be referenced.) For further investigation of the Egyptian origins of the aretalogies, see J. Bergmann's work, *Ich bin Isis: Studien zum memphitischen Hintergrund der griechischen Isisaretalogien* (Historia Religionum 3; Uppsala: Acta Universitatis Upsaliensis, 1968).

10. S. Young, ed., *An Anthology of Sacred Texts by and about Women* (New York: Crossroad, 1994), 128.

11. Young, *Anthology of Sacred Texts*, 128.

12. However, the power of Isis should not be confined to the role of women or salvation. Rather, she is believed to exercise power over law-making, earth and heaven, fate, problems, magic, and healing.

13. See R. E. Witt, *Isis in the Ancient World* (Baltimore: John Hopkins University Press, 1971), 56-57 and 264-65.

14. A. Roullet, *The Egyptian and Egyptianizing Monuments of Imperial Rome* (Leiden: E. J. Brill, 1972), 2.

15. Roullet, *Egyptianizing Monuments*, 38.

16. H. R. Willloughby, *Pagan Regeneration: A Study of Mystery Initiations in the Graeco Roman World* (Chicago: University of Chicago, 1929), 297.

Atum — 'Complete One', 'mound of the first time'
(sand & light)

Nun

Chapter One

The Origin and Institutionalizing of the Isis Cult

Atum (or Atum as Ra)

Ennead ('nine') → *Shu (Air, Life, Space, Light)* *Tefnut (Moisture, Order)*

Nut (Sky) / *Seb (Earth) or Seb*

Isis is an Egyptian goddess who rises from the Heliopolis (or the Ennead, *ennea* from the Greek word "nine"). In the Heliopolis, Tûm-Râ, also known as Ra, or the father of the gods, gives birth to Shu and Tefnut. This pair bears Seb[1] and Nut, who give birth to Osiris, Isis, Set, and Nephthys. In order to better access the origin of Isis, this chapter will look at primary documents recording Isis: *De Iside et Osiride* by Plutarch, the account by Diodorus Siculus, and the account by Apuleius in *Metamorphoses*. Following this discussion, this chapter will assess the effects of the Isis cult in Egyptian culture as well as the powers that Isis was believed to exhibit. This includes examining Cleopatra as a personification of Isis.

(typhos)
Osiris Elder Horus Seth Isis Nephthys

THE ORIGIN OF THE ISIS CULT: PRIMARY DOCUMENTS

Plutarch's Account

Plutarch provides a history of Isis and Osiris in *De Iside et Osiride*, but his account is prefaced with warnings of his deficiency in Egyptology.[2] No record exists of his length of stay on the occasion when he visits Egypt or of the amount of information he learns. Plutarch is not a contemporary of the period when the myths of Osiris originate since he is born before AD 50 and dies after AD 120.[3] His two sources of information when composing his account of Isis and Osiris are "books and priests."[4]

Although Plutarch's account is not flawless, it will be presented here since "no other work by a Greek writer is more frequently referred to by Egyptologists."[5] The Egyptian accounts of Isis and Osiris have been found to be "disconnected," making a complete account of the myth unavailable,[6] but Plutarch's account is seen as the "most coherent."[7] Plutarch's account is often

Plutarch - Greek moral essayist (early 2nd century)
Lucius Apuleius - North African Platonist — initiate + devotee of Isis. first extant Latin text

presented with a corresponding disclaimer, such as that by Egyptologist Sir
W. Budge, in which Plutarch misidentifies the Egyptian gods with those of
the Greeks and "adds a number of statements that rest either upon his own
imagination, or are the results of misinformation."[8]

With the above stated, Plutarch's account can now be discussed and ana-
lyzed.[9] Plutarch's history is written for Lady Clea but has become a "famous
treatise."[10] Plutarch begins by recounting that Osiris is the child of Cronus
and Rhea and is born on the first day of the five intercalated days of the Egyptian year.[11] He has siblings named Arueris, Typhon (known as Set in Egypt),
Isis, and Nephthys. Typhon and Nephthys join together as do Isis and Osiris
who fall in love while still in the womb.

Osiris reigns as king, and one of his first duties is to introduce a new
manner of life for the Egyptians, sparing them from "their destitute and brut-
ish manner of living."[12] Osiris does this by teaching the Egyptians to grow
crops, laying down laws for them, and showing them how to worship the
gods. He develops their civilization by traveling from place to place. During
his absence, watchful Isis stands guard (over the throne) which ensures that
Typhon behaves himself. But when Osiris returns, Typhon becomes devious
and secretly plots against Osiris.

During a festivity (perhaps a celebration was held because of the return of
Osiris), Typhon presents a lavishly decorated chest and "jestingly promised to
present it to the man who should find the chest to be exactly his length" upon
lying in it.[13] However, no man fits into the chest until Osiris climbs in. The
dimensions of the chest fit the proportions of Osiris's body perfectly because
sly Typhon has secretly measured his body and makes the chest for this sole
purpose. When Osiris lies down in it, the conspirators hurriedly secure the lid
and deposit it into the river.

When Isis hears of the news, she immediately cuts off a piece of her hair
and dons a mourning garment. She then begins a quest to find her beloved
husband. Plutarch records, "Isis wandered everywhere at her wits' end; no
one whom she approached did she fail to address."[14] When Isis speaks to
some children she learns the whereabouts of the chest which has journeyed
into the sea.

Isis also discovers that Osiris has exchanged sexual relations with Nephthys in his mistaken belief that she was Isis, which results in the birth of
a child. But because Nephthys fears Typhon, she has nothing to do with the
child, and he is forced to fend for himself. Isis then comes to the rescue of
the child and rears it, naming him Anubis, who becomes her "guardian and
attendant."[15]

Isis later learns that the chest is located near Byblus, and she travels there.
When she encounters the coffin of her husband, Isis grieves passionately over
him, even hurling herself upon his coffin and wailing excessively. Her wail-

ing is so intense that a person actually dies. When Isis is able to find a private place, she opens the coffin and "laid her face" upon that of Osiris, "caressed it and wept."[16]

Then Isis meets with her son Horus and stashes the chest in a remote location. But this location is no match for Typhon since he discovers it while hunting at night. He rips the dead body into fourteen pieces and scatters them. When Isis learns of this, she searches for her husband's dead parts. Each time she discovers a body part of Osiris, she holds a funeral for it.[17] Unfortunately, Typhon throws the phallus of Osiris into the river and it becomes fish food, much to the dismay of Isis. Because of this belief, Egyptians do not eat the fish believed to be responsible for this misfortune. To make amends for Osiris's missing phallus, Isis makes her own replica and consecrates it, which is honored by an Egyptian festival.[18]

Later, Osiris returns from the other world and trains Horus for battle with Typhon. Horus engages in battle and proves victorious. Typhon is taken captive in chains and is delivered to Isis, who mercifully releases him from his bonds and sets him free, which enrages Horus. Horus then snatches the crown perching upon Isis's head, but Hermes comes to the aid of Isis, replacing her crown with a helmet which is similar to a cow's head.

Apparently, Typhon does not really appreciate his gift of freedom, for he boldly accuses Horus of being an illegitimate offspring. Fortunately, Hermes comes to the aid of Horus and the gods decide (after Hermes's pleading) that Horus is a legitimate child after all. Horus is also victorious since Typhon is defeated in two additional battles. The story ends with Osiris having sexual relations with Isis, resulting in the birth of Harpocrates.

While it appears that Plutarch fails to account for the resurrection of Osiris, this is an inaccurate assessment. Interpretation of Plutarch's account is required, which is provided by C. J. Bleeker, who suggests that the lamentation Isis exhibited (upon finding her dead Osiris) is significant in "Egyptian mortuary belief."[19] The lamentation is "not only a natural expression of sorrow, but it possessed also the power of a spell; it raised Osiris from the dead."[20] R. J. Getty, basing his information upon the Egyptian accounts of the myth, also believes that the mourning by Isis and her sister revived Osiris.[21]

Apuleius's Account

Information regarding initiation into the Isis cult is scant at best, but the primary source is *Metamorphoses*,[22] the account of the devotee Lucius being initiated into the Isiac religion.

Metamorphoses describes a Greek named Lucius who is changed into a donkey due to his dabbling in magic. Fortunately, Isis rescues Lucius and she transforms him back into a human; Lucius, in turn, becomes an initiate of Isis.

Despite being recognized as fictitious, this account of Lucius is held in high regard by Isiac scholars.[23] E. Fantham classifies *Metamorphoses* as "the devotional finale in which Lucius the Donkey is rescued from his self-imposed transformation by the grace of Isis, to end his adventures in pious procession to her mysteries."[24] J. A. Hanson describes the account as almost a type of religious propaganda for the purpose of thanking Isis and persuading the reader to conversion.[25]

Book 11 of *Metamorphoses* begins with the plight of Lucius, who is troubled by his form of a donkey and beseeches Isis for help. She is thought to be the one with the power to change his situation. Previous to calling upon the goddess, Lucius purifies himself in the sea, dunking his head underneath the water a total of seven times. Lucius prays for rest from the cruelties of life and for an improvement of his fortune. He has suffered enough as a donkey and prays to Isis for deliverance.

After he is finished praying to Isis, Lucius sleeps. But when he closes his eyes, he encounters the beautiful face of Isis, and finds himself at a loss to begin to describe her. However, he makes an honest attempt in recounting her long locks and her detailed crown. Isis's crown encompasses many aspects of her deity: being decorated with flowers, a mirror resembling the moon (in the middle of the crown), snakes (which flank the crown), and ears of wheat (above her crown). Isis also wears a robe of many colors which is not to be outdone by her glistening black cloak[26] adorned with stars (with moons in the middle of them). "A garland of flowers and fruits" is also attached to her garment.[27]

The prayers of Lucius are answered as Isis speaks, revealing her true identity to him. She describes herself as the "mother of the universe, mistress of all the elements, and first offspring of the ages" to name a few of her titles.[28] While she is one "divinity," people worship her by different names throughout the world.[29] Apuleius lists the many names of Isis used by various peoples, which ends with the Egyptians who call her Queen Isis. Isis is compassionate toward Lucius and she tells him not to cry anymore because his deliverance is coming.

The next day is proclaimed as belonging to Isis "by everlasting religious observance."[30] On this day, once the sea settles and the winds quiet, the ceremony would begin. The priests would dedicate an "untried keel [or new boat] to the now navigable sea and consecrate it as the first fruits of voyaging."[31] Another priest of Isis would have "a garland of roses attached to the sistrum."[32] Lucius is told to pass through the crowd to get to the priest participating in the procession. When he reaches the priest, Lucius is instructed to "pluck the roses" and shed his animal form.[33] Isis promises her presence to Lucius and that her plans would be revealed to the priest in his sleep about the proper course of action. Isis then assures Lucius that the people would allow him to pass through to the priest despite his hideous form, and that he would not be penalized when the transformation took place.[34]

The rest of Lucius's days are to be "pledged" to Isis until his dying day.[35] But Isis informs Lucius, "you will live in happiness, you will live in glory, under my guardianship."[36] When Lucius dies, he will journey down under the earth and be reunited with Isis. Her favor will be bestowed upon him and he will pay devotion to her through continual worship. If he excels in his worship, obedience, and celibacy to procure the favor of Isis's "godhead," Isis will enable his life to be extended "beyond the limits" of his fate.[37]

Following the revelation from Isis, Lucius then awakens and is taken aback from his encounter with her. Using "sea spray," he "sprinkled" himself and eagerly awaits the day of his deliverance.[38] Suddenly the next day arrives in all its grandeur and glory. The festivities start with individuals in various costumes parading, followed by the "special procession of the savior goddess."[39] Women adorned in white scatter flowers for the "sacred company" who would follow.[40] Others express their appreciation for the goddess through dispersing ointments, bearing mirrors (to honor Isis), and carrying combs (to "comb" Isis's hair). People also pay homage to Isis by carrying candles and other light-bearing objects to honor Isis since she is believed to be the "source of the heavenly stars."[41] These acts are followed by melodies sung by pipes and flutes, and youth singing a hymn with "interim preludes to the 'Greater Vows.' "[42]

Following the youth are the pipers who have pled their allegiance to Sarapis and show their appreciation to him through their melody.[43] The initiated are the next to follow in the procession, all using their sistrums to make a "shrill ringing sound."[44] The initiated men display their shiny, shaven heads representative of the "earthly stars" of the Isis religion.[45] Following the initiates are the high priests, clothed in white, holding various objects which are representative of the gods. The first priest lugs a "golden boat"[46] which functions as a luminous lamp. The second priest bears an altar or a "source of help," symbolizing Isis as the one to help humankind.[47] Other objects in the procession include a golden-leafed palm branch, a caduceus (that resembled the winged staff of Mercury), a symbol of justice, a breast-shaped vessel from which milk is poured, a "golden winnowing-fan," and an oval vessel with two handles (also known as an amphora).[48]

The gods trail behind the high priests. First is Anubis (or the messenger of the gods), who is followed by a cow, or the "fertile symbol of the divine mother of all."[49] Secret objects hidden in a basket are also carried in the procession as well as the image of Isis that takes the form of an urn which is decorated with "Egyptian images."[50]

The priest then advances toward Lucius and Lucius cautiously works his way through the mass of people toward him. The priest, who Lucius believes carries his "destiny" and "salvation" holds a "sistrum" for Isis and a "crown of victory" to bestow upon Lucius.[51] The crown is seen as appropriate for Lucius due to the many trials he has suffered during the course of his life. But Lucius's trials are about to end, for he would soon "overcome Fortune" by the help of Isis.[52]

From Lucius's perspective, the priest remembers the instructions given to him in a dream from Isis. He clutches a wreath of roses for Lucius to eat, which he devours and is instantly transformed. He hastily sheds his hideous form and regains his human form. Astonishment strikes the crowd and the followers of Isis praise her. Lucius is elated at his new form and finds himself without words. He is provided a tunic from one of Isis's devotees and clothes himself appropriately. The priest then addresses Lucius in what is described as a "prophetic utterance."[53] In short, despite the trials that he has endured in his life, he has "reached the harbour of Peace and the altar of Mercy."[54] While he has suffered at the cruel hands of Fortune, he has now been redeemed due to Isis, who has rescued him from his trials, safeguarded him, and liberated him under her protection.

Lucius is then encouraged to be happy and take part in the procession. He will serve as an example to those who do not believe in Isis. But he is also urged to express a greater allegiance to Isis through obedience and service. Lucius then joins in the procession and becomes an example of the transforming power of Isis and is consequently the talk of the crowd. People remark that he is "in a manner *reborn* and immediately engaged to the service of her [Isis's] cult."[55]

"reborn"

The procession then advances to the shoreline where the ceremony continues. In the presence of the "images of the gods,"[56] (perhaps as witnessing the event), the chief priest of Isis commences the ceremony. Then the events (which might be more accurately described as the *Navigium Isidis*) are recorded, beginning with the consecration of a ship (decorated with Egyptian pictures) by the chief priest. The chief priest prays over the ship and purifies it before naming and dedicating the ship to Isis. The ship is complete with an inscription "whose text renewed the prayer for prosperous navigation during the new sailing season."[57]

After the consecration of the ship, the initiated and the uninitiated pay homage to Isis by hoisting their offerings onto the ship. Then, offerings of "grain-mash made with milk"[58] are poured out upon the waves of the sea. Once these rituals are complete, the ship is freed from its ties and presented to the sea.

Once the ship practically vanishes from sight, the party of people retreat back to the shrine in typical procession format. Once at the temple, selected individuals are gathered into the private chamber of Isis. These include the initiates of the inner sanctuary, those who have paraded with the objects in the

(high priests)

procession, and the chief priest. The scribe of this group then calls together the "*pastophori*" which translates as "shrine-bearers."[59] Prayers are then pronounced for the governing authorities (the emperor and senate), the Romans, *prayers* and those involved in sea-faring (sailors and ships),[60] which are followed by a official proclamation that begins the season of navigation. The crowd accepts this proclamation and pays homage to Isis by kissing her feet and showering her with foliage.[61]

The word of Lucius's deliverance spreads throughout the land. His friends (who thought that he has been dead) rejoice in his newly-found life. After Lucius testifies to them, he takes great joy in the "contemplation" of Isis.[62] He resides in a house which he rents in the "temple precinct," devotes himself to the worship of Isis, and serves her as a lay person.[63] Every time Lucius lies down to sleep, Isis speaks to him through visions and orders him to be initiated. However, Lucius is hesitant in doing so because he knows of the obligations attached to the cult, such as chastity.

Lucius then has a dream where the chief priest gives gifts to him, which are shares (probably from an inheritance)[64] from Thessaly. In this dream, Lucius has a slave named Candidus who travels from this place to meet Lucius. However, Lucius has never had a slave called Candidus and is puzzled with the perplexity of the interpretation of this dream and awaits its proper meaning. He then goes to the temple and attends the "morning opening" where prayer is offered to the image of Isis.[65] A priest prays and sprinkles water from a vessel and visits the various altars in the temple. Lucius is then met by some servants who bring back his white horse. The white horse is recognized as the prophetic meaning of the name Candidus, meaning "white."[66]

After this event, Lucius yearns to become initiated into the cult of Isis and beseeches the high priest to initiate him. The deeply religious high priest politely tries to discourage Lucius from becoming an initiate and informs him that initiation day was "marked by a nod" from Isis.[67] Isis also engineers other details relating to initiation, such as the choice of a priest and the exact cost. Initiation is to proceed with caution for if the priest initiates an individual without Isis's directive, he will be punished. The chief priest explains to Lucius, "Both the gates of death and the guardianship of life *rebirth* were in the goddess's hands, and the act of initiation was performed in the manner of voluntary death and salvation obtained by favour."[68] Furthermore, those who can be entrusted with the secret mysteries are enabled to be "reborn through her providence and set once more upon the course of renewed life."[69] Lucius is encouraged to start regulating his diet by avoiding "unholy and unlawful foods" in order to more properly enter into the mysteries of Isis.[70]

Lucius continues to perform his service to the goddess on a daily basis, celebrating the rites of Isis. One night, Isis speaks to Lucius, telling him that

ed day of his initiation has arrived. The price of the ceremonies is
to Lucius, and Mithras (the high priest of Isis), is responsible for
out the initiation process. Upon receiving these instructions, Lucius
rushes over to the apartment of the priest. The priest recognizes how fortunate
Lucius is to obtain favor in the eyes of Isis. Mithras confirms to Lucius that
his day of initiation has now arrived and he will be introduced into the secrets
of the Isis cult.

Lucius is then led to the great temple by the high priest. After the morning
rituals, the high priest brings out some books with "unknown characters."[71]
The high priests[72] then read the "preparations" for the initiation process.[73]
Evidently the words from the preparations for the initiation require purchas-
ing objects, which Lucius does (or has his friends purchase them).

Next the priest takes him to the baths in the presence of the devotees of Isis.
Lucius comments, "When I had taken the customary bath,[74] he [the priest]
began by asking the gods' favour and then cleansed me with purificatory
sprinkling."[75] Following the sprinkling, Lucius is escorted to the feet of Isis in
the back of the temple. Secret instructions are given to Lucius and he is told
to observe dietary regulations for ten days (specifically, to abstain from wine
and "animal food"),[76] which he dutifully obeys.

The day arrives for Lucius to appear before the gods. As dusk approaches,
Lucius is surrounded by a crowd of people and is showered with gifts. Those
who have not been initiated into the Isis cult are requested to leave. Lucius is
then dressed in a linen garment[77] and is led by the priest into the inner sanctuary. Lucius then shrouds some of his initiation account in secrecy. Nevertheless, he does relent and recounts his journey, traveling to the "boundary of
death" and "the threshold of Proserpina [a goddess of underworld/death],"[78]
which can be understood as simply a metaphor for death.[79] He then journeys
"through all the elements" and encounters the brilliant sun as well as the gods
below and above, whom Lucius honors.

Lucius then gives a disclaimer about the rest of his account, for he can only
speak what is appropriate for the "uninitiated without atonement."[80]   Morning follows and after the completion of the ceremonies Lucius emerges and
is clothed with twelve robes[81] "as a sign of consecration," and he stands in
front of the statue atop a platform in the shrine.[82] He also wears a garment,
which is coined as the "Olympian stole" and a cloak.[83] He carries a torch,
and a luminous crown is placed upon his head. The adornment that Lucius
receives resembles the appearance of "the Sun," and he is put on display for
the gaze of the people.[84] Lucius then celebrates his "birth into the mysteries"
by a "delicious banquet and a cheerful party."[85] The third day also resembles
the same fashion with a "sacred breakfast," and the conclusion of the initiation occurs.[86] Lucius stays for a few days and then plans to head homeward.
He leaves his payment of gratitude to Isis.

Becoming Christ

Then he falls forward before her, and sobbing on occasion, prays to the goddess. He addresses her as "holy and eternal saviour," and one who offers the "sweet affection of a mother to the misfortunes of the wretched."[87] Her blessings abound for humankind on a daily basis. Lucius continues his adoration to Isis, praising her for her protection of people whether on earth or sea, for her victory over Fate and Fortune, and her dominance over the elements of the universe (i.e. stars, seasons, seeds, etc.). Lucius then embraces Mithras, expresses his thanks to him, and returns home. He then journeys to Rome at the command of Isis and arrives at the "Port of Augustus" and becomes an attendant at the temple of Isis (the Campus Martius) located in Rome.[88]

While the Lucius account is fictitious in respect to his transformation from a donkey to a person, the descriptive aspects of initiation are based upon facts. Since facts undergird the fictitious elements, its genre may be classified as a historical narrative. A few examples will suffice for my purposes. For instance, the temple where Lucius is initiated has been described as an Iseum at Cenchraea.[89] Furthermore, the water pitcher in the account is "one of the most important familiar objects in Isis-worship" and has been matched by evidence in Iseums.[90] Finally, historical references exist in this account, such as the Campus Martius and the Port of Augustus; the ceremony of the *Navigium Isidis* is also detailed.

Diodorus Siculus's Account

In his account, Diodorus Siculus records that the men of Egypt are in awe of their universe when they first come into being many years ago. The impression of their surroundings leads them to believe in the existence of two eternal deities: the sun (also known as Osiris) and the moon (also called Isis).[91] These names, Osiris and Isis, are based upon their corresponding meaning which relates to their roles. Osiris explores the earth and water with his eyes (also seen to parallel the far-reaching rays of the sun); true to his namesake, Osiris is defined as "many-eyed" in Greek.[92] Diodorus cites Homer's line from the *Odyssey* to validate his view of Osiris, saying, "The sun, who sees all things and hears all things,"[93] which gives a fuller illustration of the role of Osiris.

The name of Isis is translated as "ancient" to describe her birth being so long ago.[94] The idea of the moon in reference to Isis is incorporated by the horns which are attached onto Isis's head. These horns resemble the crescent moon as well as the cow (an animal sacred to the goddess).[95]

Osiris and Isis have a unique role for they "regulate the entire universe, giving both nourishment and increase to all things" in the seasons of spring, summer, and winter.[96] These two deities are essentially the backbone of existence for they provide "practically all the physical matter which is essential to the generation of all things."[97] Osiris as the sun furnishes the "fiery element and the spirit" while Isis as the moon provides the "wet and the dry."[98] Both Osiris and Isis combined are responsible for supplying the air.[99] Other parts of the earth are known by different names of gods and goddesses; for example, the earth is seen as Demeter.[100]

Following the discussion of other gods and goddesses, Diodorus describes some gods and goddesses who, although once mortals, earn immortality because of their benevolent actions to humankind. Some of these are kings in Egypt, such as Helius, Cronus, Rhea, Zeus (who is known as Ammon), Hera, Hephaestus, Hestia, and Hermes. Hephaestus is thought to be the first king of the Egyptians, but Cronus later takes his place as ruler. Cronus marries his sister Rhea, and Osiris and Isis are born. However, the more popular opinion is that Zeus and Hera are born to Cronus and Rhea. Zeus and Rhea give birth to a total of five gods and goddesses, each born on the five days inserted at the end of the year[101] after the Egyptian calendar of 360 days. These gods and goddesses include Osiris, Isis, Typhon, Apollo, and Aphrodite.

Osiris and Isis have variant names according to Diodorus. Osiris is known as Dionysus when his name is translated; Isis bears similarities to the goddess Demeter.[102] Osiris marries Isis and becomes king and improves the life of the common person.[103] Among Osiris's accomplishments is the abolishment of the practice of cannibalism. People are happy to forsake this pursuit and alter their dietary habits after Isis "discovered the fruit of both wheat and barley," which is unknown to people prior to this occurrence.[104] Osiris also takes fair share in this discovery for he engineers the "cultivation of these fruits."[105]

People dedicate the "first heads of the grain to be cut,"[106] which is a way to pay homage to Isis. While "standing beside the sheaf [they] beat themselves and call upon Isis" and consequently honor her for her discovery of the grains.[107] Other means of honoring Isis include people bearing bundles of wheat and barley in the Festival of Isis, which remind others of her accomplishment.[108] Isis is also known as a lawgiver besides being a goddess of agriculture for she is thought to establish laws to uphold justice and prohibit illegal behavior.[109]

Diodorus also gives considerable attention to Osiris in his account. Osiris, also known as Dionysus, is raised in Nysa. Like Isis, Osiris also has a strong connection with agriculture. He discovers the vine (and also wine) and imparts his wisdom to others, teaching them such aspects of wine-making as how to "harvest the grape and to store the wine."[110] He draws a "great army"[111] to himself for the purpose of journeying around the land to accomplish this pursuit as well as instructing them how to "sow wheat and barley."[112]

Before embarking on this venture, he ultimately surrenders his rule of Egypt to his wife for he hands the "supreme power over to Isis."[113] His campaign is beneficial for he enhances "community life by the introduction of the fruits" which benefit humankind.[114] When returning to Egypt, Osiris brings great presents and is granted immortality and honour like that bestowed upon the heavenly gods. He then enters the "company of the gods" and rites are instituted for Osiris.[115]

Despite Osiris's accomplishments, he cannot overcome the evil plot of his brother Typhon. Typhon murders the king of Egypt and divides his body into twenty-six pieces, which are distributed to his accomplices. Typhon disposes of the undesirable parts (or his "privates") into the river of the Nile.[116] Isis makes up for this misfortune by forming a replica of Osiris's parts and placing it in the temples. She demands honor and reverence in the devotion given to Osiris.[117]

As for the other parts of Osiris, Diodorus records Isis's actions: "Over each piece of the body, as the account goes, she fashioned out of spices and wax a human figure about the size of Osiris."[118] She then gathers each group of priests together individually, and after they take an oath not to betray her confidence, only then does she tell them that they alone are responsible for Osiris's body. They are to "bury his body in their own district and pay honours to him as to a god"[119] as well as consecrate animals to Osiris and honor them as they would normally honor the husband of Isis. When the animals die, they are to mourn for their death as they would mourn for Osiris. The priests are obedient to follow the directives of Isis.

The rest of Isis's days are spent reigning over Egypt abiding by the laws of the land and giving gifts to the people. She also refuses to remarry. When Isis herself dies, she receives "immortal honour" and is buried near Memphis.[120]

Diodorus also notes the many accomplishments of Isis in the Egyptian mindset. Isis is known for discovering drugs that contribute to the health of humankind. She is also a goddess who specializes in healing and takes great joy in alleviating the ills of humankind. One particular oddity in Isis's healing is that she dispatches her help when people are asleep. Diodorus comments, "For standing above the sick in their sleep she gives them aid for diseases and works remarkable cures upon such as submit themselves to her."[121]

Her wonder-working powers, such as the restoration of eyes or body parts, are impressive for she heals the problem cases that doctors are often at a loss to help. But better than physical healing is the gift (or drug) of immortality which she offers as an immortal goddess. Her son Horus, who also becomes king,[122] is a recipient of this gift, for Isis raises him from the dead and restores him to an immortal state.

In conclusion, examining the primary sources that chronicle the account of Isis are critical for developing a basis for Isiac theology. Isiac theology might be described as the beliefs about Isis that became prevalent in Egyptian culture, and later in Greco-Roman culture. The primary sources also help illustrate how Egyptian culture, in particular, views Isis. While the accounts are by no means foolproof, they are excellent foundational material. Without appreciating the accounts by Plutarch, Apuleius, and Diodorus Siculus, one would be at a loss to grasp the ideals of the Isis cult. Of equal importance, however, are the effects that the Isis cult imprinted upon Egyptian culture.

THE EFFECTS OF THE ISIS CULT IN EGYPTIAN CULTURE

Analysis of the primary sources is important when determining the impact that Isis exerts upon Egyptian culture. The thoughts surrounding Isis as recorded in the primary documents evolved from written material into a theology. This "theology" is alluded to in the section that follows, which speaks of the "power" that Isis supposedly exhibits over humankind.[123]

Power of Isis Over Women and Marriage

One of the greatest insights into the power that Isis supposedly holds over a marriage relationship is stated explicitly in *Papyrus Oxyrhynchus XI.1380*, dating from the early second century AD. It reads, "thou [Isis] did make the power of women equal to that of men."[124] This simple statement among other details of Isiac myths, has contributed to an Isiac theology involving Isis as the "self-proclaimed leader of the movement for the emancipation of women."[125] Isis herself serves an example for women to follow through filling the vacancy of Osiris on the throne. In doing so, she partakes of full power as equivalent to that of her husband as king. However, this principle does not apply to Isis alone, but she extends it to women to "enjoy authority over their husbands."[126]

Isis is also the protector of her husband. This is evident from the following inscription, taken from a limestone stela, dating from 1567–1320 BC or the Eighteenth Dynasty:

> His [Osiris'] sister [Isis][127] was his guard,
> She who drives off the foes,
> Who stops the deeds of the disturber
> By the power of her utterance.
> The clever-tongued whose speech fails not,
> Effective in the word of command,
> Mighty Isis who protected her brother,
> Who sought him without wearying.[128]

This inscription or hymn "contains the fullest account of the Osiris myth extant in Egyptian, as distinct from Greek, sources."[129] Evident from this inscription, Isis has taken the dominant role in the relationship between her and her husband. Generally speaking, the man would protect the woman. However, in the case of Isis, this role is reversed. Isis protects her husband, being his guard and his defender.

Another example (from the hymn of Andros) shows that Isis had the power to make the wife obedient to the leading of her husband.[130] However, because the husband relies not upon command, but upon persuasion, this would not truly be considered to be a solid example of the husband really having the lead in the marriage. The status of the wife is higher than that of the husband because of the means of persuasion being used. If the status of the wife would be inferior to that of her husband, then command would be utilized.

Isis is also described as "the model par excellence for married life."[131] From a literary standpoint, Isis upholds the institution of marriage as she devises marriage contracts in the Kyme Aretalogy. The dynamics of relationships between men and women are also encouraged by Isis for she claims to have "brought together woman and man" and "compelled women to be loved by men."[132] She also strengthens the family unit for she "ordained that parents should be loved by their children."[133]

From a mythological standpoint, Isis is a shining example of a devoted spouse. For instance, she perseveres in her marriage with Osiris despite all odds.[134] Even though Osiris apparently struggles in his faithfulness toward her since he "accidentally" sleeps with her sister (causing the birth of a child), Isis does not swerve in her devotion to her beloved spouse.[135] After his death, she searches everywhere for her dearest Osiris and vows not to marry another man. She also slays the evil Typhon and his wicked accomplices (with the help of her son) before rising to the throne as queen of Egypt. Osiris can ask for nothing more in his wife for Isis goes above and beyond her call of duty in her dedication to her husband. While Isis is known for a myriad of roles, "her dominant trait was her loving devotion to Osiris and her motherly love for Horus."[136]

Power of Isis in Law-Making

The scope of Isis's power is not limited to empowering women in their relationships with men. Rather, it extends into the power of the government as well for Isis is known as "the Lawgiver."[137] In essence, she is the one who is responsible for establishing the laws and she has a particular emphasis on law and order. Isis gets her opportunity to prove herself after the death of Osiris. She reigns over Egypt in a law-abiding manner and is also identified as the cause of blessings upon humankind.[138]

Isis exerts her power in law-making above that of men. Unlike the laws of men which might be described as fickle (or subject to change), the laws of

Isis might be hypothetically characteri   olid or steadfast (not subject to change). This is apparent from Diodor   writes of the following inscription on a stele: "I am Isis, the queen or every land, she who was instructed of Hermes, and whatsoever laws I have established, these can no man make void."[139] From this quotation, it is clear the type of power that Isis desires and is believed to possess over humankind.

Besides being the Lawgiver, the Kyme Aretalogy attests: "I [Isis] broke down the governments of tyrants."[140] This statement is noteworthy since it is left to question how much of this statement is directly influenced by the personal experiences of Isis. Does this thought originate from the practice of Isis ruling when her husband dies? How does she view the behavior of Osiris when he is in power? Whether or not Isis judges the behavior of her husband in government as tyrannical is uncertain.

Power of Isis in Earth and Heaven

Again, the power of Isis is not limited to one sector of life, but her power encompasses a broader scope. Not only is she believed to take precedence over the affairs of humankind, but she is also considered to exercise power upon earth and in the heavenly realm. On earth, Isis is identified as the "maternal life force."[141] For example, Isis is seen as a giver of life to her son and her husband for she makes them immortal.[142] In terms of the activities of the heavens, Isis is identified as the "queen of heaven."[143] This title expresses her dominance in the heavenly realm; Isis is also known as "greatest of the gods."[144]

Isis also exercises her authority over the sun, winds, and water. The Kyme Aretalogy reads: "I [Isis] am the Queen of rivers and winds and sea. . . . I am the Queen of the thunderbolt. I stir up the sea and I calm it. I am in the rays of the sun. I inspect the course of the sun."[145] Isis continues, speaking of her dominance over the sea, "I [Isis] devised business in the sea."[146] Furthermore, "I [Isis] am the Queen of seamanship. I make the navigable unnavigable *when it pleases me*."[147] Statements like these may have provoked fear among the sailors (for the sea was their primary means of transportation) and may have been the underlying reason why they would pay devotion to Isis.[148] If Isis is appeased, sea-faring will supposedly be uneventful.

Besides taking precedence in heaven and in earth, Isis plays an important role in the activity between heaven and earth. The Kyme Aretalogy reveals the words of Isis concerning these activities as follows: "I divided the earth from the heaven. I showed the paths of the stars. I ordered the course of the sun and the moon."[149] Isis's realm of influence also extends into the sphere of creation. In Apuleius's account, Isis is equated with the stars and the sun. The cloak of Isis contains stars which have flaming moons in their centers.[150] Also, in the Isiac procession, the men initiated into the Isis cult display their shiny shaven heads as representative of the "earthly stars" of the Isis cult.[151] This is in addition to those who carry light-bearing objects (such as lamps, torches, candles) to honor Isis as the one who gives light to the stars.[152] Diodorus also touches on Isis's function in creation by highlighting her role as a fertility goddess, particularly in the crop of grain[153] and equating her with the moon.[154] These primary accounts can be supplemented with statements from the Kyme Aretalogy. For example, the Kyme Aretalogy reads, "I [Isis] am in the rays of the sun. I inspect the courses of the sun."

Power of Isis Over Fate

Besides Isis exercising her power over earth and heaven, Isis also has power over fate, thus demonstrating her sovereignty. Her superiority over fate is attested to in The Kyme Aretalogy. It reads, "I [Isis] overcome Fate. Fate harkens to me."[155] Whatever Isis desires to happen will happen, according to Isis. She states, "Whatever I please, this too shall come to an end."[156] While this may have a positive connotation, this can also have destructive consequences for those who are not in her favor, contributing to the worship of Isis by her followers.

Power of Isis in Salvation

Isis is also thought to demonstrate her influence in salvific activity. R. E. Witt remarks, "She [Isis] resurrected. The gates of Hell, besides salvation were in her hands."[157] However, L. LiDonnici clarifies Witt's statement by limiting the salvation of Isis solely to initiates of the Isis cult,[158] which does not include everyone. Rather, salvation is a "function of initiation into one or more religions, usually called *mysteries*, which brought the initiate into an intimate and permanent relationship with a particular deity."[159] Superficial relationships with pagan deities do not merit salvation. Salvation occurs after death when the deity rescues the individual's soul from the "rather miserable place of the dead" and brought it into "a place of happiness."[160]

Power of Isis Over Problems

Despite the fact that the salvation granted by Isis is limited in terms of its scope, salvation or deliverance from the trials of life may be given to all calling upon her. LiDonnici states, "Isis helped anyone who called upon her, both women and men, in any area of trouble, from childbirth to shipwreck."[161] Isis alleviates people from the problems of their lives since she is available to meet people's requests for help, assistance, or intervention. Just as she does not turn a deaf ear to Lucius, she does not turn a deaf ear to humankind.

Because of this characteristic of Isis, Isis remains distinct from other deities. "The great majority of ancient saviors offered only eternal blessedness and were totally unconcerned with the events before death."[162] Isis is an exception to the norm for she offers help to people in the midst of their earthly lives, thus exhibiting compassion upon the plights of humanity. If other gods or goddesses do exhibit a certain degree of compassion, it is generally confined "as a transportation of the soul away from the pain of human life" rather than trying to better a person's situation.[163] The compassionate nature of Isis can only have increased the enticement of this goddess and her corresponding cult for she is described as "gentle" and "affectionate" as well as a "giver of favors."[164]

Isis: Goddess of Magic and Healing

In addition to the power of Isis as detailed above, Isis is also known as "the great sorceress"[165] and possesses magical abilities. Horus, her son, is called the "son of an enchantress."[166] The magical power of Isis is exhibited in the myths surrounding her, most particularly in the story surrounding her and Ra, where Isis inflicts pain upon Ra but later alleviates his pain by means of a spell. A myth also exists where Horus is conceived by the means of spells.[167]

Isis is also believed to be responsible for the "art of medicine."[168] From the Egyptian mindset, Isis is the goddess who discovers drugs that give health to humankind.[169] Besides medicinal intervention, she is "an expert in making men well when they betook themselves to her temple, where after incubation they could look forward in hope to gain a cure."[170] Through the healings that Isis gives, her kindness is manifested. It is also marveled that she heals those physicians cannot,[171] which may have helped her earn the "unswerving love and loyalty of countless men and women" in the Greco-Roman world.[172]

Spells document the magical powers of Isis. Isis is contacted in order to protect bodies after they are dead. For example, Budge records one spell of Isis. It reads as follows: "The blood of Isis, the power of Isis, the words of power of Isis shall be strong to protect this mighty sick one (*i.e.* the mummy), and to guard him from him that would do unto him anything which he abominateth (or, is taboo to him)."[173] Specific steps are also taken in the course of the spell. However, the significance underlying the magic of Isis is that it helps enhance her popular appeal— to possess power over the fate of the dead and their prospective journeys is a rarity.

Isis in Egyptian History

As an Egyptian goddess, Isis performs a critical role in Egyptian history. Her character, as noted above, encompasses a variety of roles.[174] One of these roles, of significance to Egypt, is to guarantee the "fertility of fields and the abundance of harvests."[175] Diodorus links Isis to Demeter because of her similarities to this grain goddess, which also gives a clear indication of Isis's role in agriculture.[176] The Egyptians honor this goddess when they harvest the grain as well as publicly recognize her role in agriculture in the procession of the Festival of Isis.[177] Agriculture is of critical importance in Egypt for "wheat and barley bread" constitute the "staple foods" of this country.[178]

Another one of her roles, equally as important as a goddess of agriculture, is her role in the raising of the Nile.[179] The sorrow of Isis, overflowing into her tears, is the popular belief as to what constitutes the rise of the Nile.[180] The fall of the Nile is also credited to Isis for she "bringest back the Nile over every country."[181] The ties that Isis has to the Nile, which is essentially the backbone of Egyptian life, illustrate her importance in the Egyptian mindset.[182]

While Isis plays an integral role in both agriculture and the Nile, she also impacts Egyptian society in terms of its relationships between men and women. The example that Isis sets in mythology becomes a blueprint for Egyptian culture. Diodorus explains this phenomenon,

> The Egyptians also made a law, they say, contrary to the general custom of mankind, permitting men to marry their sisters, *this being due to the success attained by Isis in this respect*; for she had married her brother Osiris, and upon his death, having taken a vow never to marry another man, she both avenged the murder of her husband and reigned all her days over the land with complete respect for the laws, and, in a word, became the cause of more and greater blessings to all men than any other. It is for these reasons, in fact, that *it was ordained that the queen should have greater power and honour than the king and that among private persons the wife should enjoy authority over her husband, the husbands agreeing in the marriage contract that they will be obedient in all things to their wives.*[183]

In addition to Diodorus, Sophocles also illustrates the effects that Isis had upon society in *Oedipus at Colonus*, which illuminates the mannerisms and behaviors of the Egyptians.[184] Concerning the Egyptians, the customary roles of men and women are reversed as the play of *Oedipus at Colonus* demonstrates:

> Their thoughts and actions all
> Are framed and modelled on Egyptian ways
> For there the men sit at the loom indoors
> While the wives slave abroad for daily bread.[185]

This work is further evidence of the effect of the Isis cult upon Egyptian society.

Isis as Promoted by Government

The Isis cult is not just something in which private citizens took interest; rather, the Isis cult is promoted by the government. The government, particularly the Ptolemies (323-30 BC), made use of religion to further their political agenda and to increase the popularity of their reign.[186] The rationale for supporting Isis was as follows: "Since Isis, Osiris, and Horus were the mythical *divine order* guarantors of divine order it was inevitable that the Ptolemies would capitalize on this tradition to secure their political power and to build a popular base of support."[187] The "steady erosion of Egyptian traditions by aggressive Hellenization policies" necessitate the need for action.[188]

Nevertheless, the efforts to secure the political arena by those in power comes into conflict in the second century. At this time, "the power of the hierarchy was waxing and that of the monarchy waning."[189] Because of this, those in power want to increase their support for the gods and goddesses so that this popularity would overflow to them. "Huge sums of money" were used to enlarge the temples, particularly under Ptolemy Philadelphus (285-246 BC) who constructs "a great temple of Isis in the delta and one at Philae."[190]

Egyptian rulers, such as Seti,[191] would issue a decree and then call upon the gods to enforce it. In the case of Seti, he appoints a group of gold-washers to the House of *Menmare*; he wants this group to be protected and to stay true to their duties. "As to anyone who shall interfere with any of them so as to put them in another place, all the gods and goddesses of my [Seti's] House shall be his adversaries."[192] Furthermore, "As to anyone who shall be deaf to this decree, Osiris shall be after him, Isis after his wife, Horus after his children; and all the great ones, the lords of the necropolis, will make their reckoning with him!"[193]

From Theory to Practice: Isis Imitated

In order to better secure the reign of those in power, the kings and queens took care to imitate the dynamics of the relationships of the family of Isis to the best of their ability. In this manner, they tried to link themselves to the gods in whatever means possible. This is especially true of the reign of the Ptolemies.

Philadelphus or Ptolemy II, in imitation of Osiris, married his sister which is a carbon copy of the relationship established by Isis and Osiris: husband and wife as brother and sister. Furthermore, Euergetes or Ptolemy III (246-221 BC) also attempts to establish a connection "between the patterns of relationship in the divine household and those in the royal family."[194] His wife, Bernice II, identifies herself with Isis.[195] In addition, Philopator or Ptolemy IV (221-203 BC) has his son "acclaimed as Horus."[196]

The practice of associating with Isis is also seen in the example of the Ptolemaic queens before Cleopatra VII who depict themselves as Isis.[197] "By linking themselves with her and invoking her sanction to rule, Ptolemaic queens like Cleopatra were able to give a semblance of legitimacy and vulnerability to the power of their dynasty, still perceived by many Egyptians as one of the foreign usurpers."[198] Identifying oneself with the cult of Isis enables the ruler to identify with the people of Egypt and establish common ground.

Cleopatra: Personification of Isis ("the new Isis")

Cleopatra identifies herself with Isis as indicative by her marriages to her brothers.[199] For instance, Ptolemy XIII, the brother as well as husband of Cleopatra, is in power as co-ruler of Egypt from 51-47 BC. The Isis cult is imitated here as Cleopatra marries her brother. She is eighteen at the time and her brother is only ten.[200] However, Ptolemy XIII is only alive for a few years in power since he is found drowned in the Nile River due to the weight of his own armor after a battle.[201] Cleopatra then marries her younger brother, Ptolemy XIV, who reigns with Cleopatra from 47-44 BC. Nevertheless, both Ptolemy XIII and Ptolemy XIV are often overshadowed by Cleopatra, given their marginal information in historical sources. They are known primarily for their association with her for Cleopatra is understood to be the one truly in power, demonstrating that she does have greater power and honor than the king.

To understand Cleopatra in her most accurate light, it is important to understand her background. Cleopatra is in power from 51-30 BC as queen of Egypt and she is productive in her endeavors as queen since she proves herself successful both in business affairs and in ruling the country of Egypt. Cleopatra proves by her "powerful intelligence, wit, and considerable political ability" that she could govern equally to that of a man.[202] In this light, it seems appropriate that coins are issued to the public of the "Queen of Kings" (or Cleopatra).[203] Antony falls for Cleopatra and divorces Octavia (Octavian's sister) to marry the Egyptian ruler.

Cleopatra helps to promote her agenda by associating herself with Isis as a means of establishing common ground with the inhabitants of Egypt. By identifying with Isis, Cleopatra bridges "the gap between the culture of her Greek-speaking court and that of her native Egyptian subjects."[204] Cleopatra is successful in her portrayal of Isis, for "in the eyes of her subjects she was Isis incarnate."[205] In order to portray herself as this goddess, she dresses in a "robe sacred to Isis."[206]

However, the question can easily be raised: Does Cleopatra take this a step further? At what point does Cleopatra stop acting as Isis and start believing she is Isis? Cleopatra is identified as the "new Isis" according to Plutarch.[207] Furthermore, Cleopatra is surrounded by a "divine aura as a reincarnation of Isis."[208] She partakes of the identity of Isis to such a degree that she is actually believed to embody Isis as Cleopatra is identified as the "avatar" of Isis on earth.[209]

The roles of the Isis cult are not limited to Cleopatra, however. Antony also participates in the cult since he is identified as Osiris. Dio Cassius records that painters and sculptors in their work portray him as Osiris (or Dionysus) with Cleopatra as Isis (or Selene).[210] To understand this association, the following may be taken into consideration:

> In the Graeco-Egyptian culture of Egypt, Osiris and Dionysus were often identified with one another as deities, and also associated with the cult of ruler-worship. The rulers of the Hellenistic kingdoms ever since the time of Alexander the Great had come to be regarded as gods on earth, gods made manifest in living beings. Antony had been received as the New Dionysus at Ephesus in 41 B.C. Cleopatra's father, Ptolemy Auletes, was referred to as the New Dionysus. The word Osiris signifies the Occupier of the Throne. On the same principle the god's partner, Isis, was often identified with the queen, whether consort or regnant, and Cleopatra followed this practice.[211]

It is because of the fact that painters and sculptors identify Osiris and Cleopatra with the corresponding deities which "more than anything else" leads to the belief that Cleopatra "had laid him [Antony] under some spell and deprived him of his wits."[212]

Upon analysis of Dio Cassius's account as written in *Roman History* (50.5.1), D. Balch writes, "The Romans were offended that Antony seemed 'enslaved' to Cleopatra."[213] F. Hooper also comments, "It was repeatedly charged in Rome that he [Antony] was too much under Cleopatra's influence."[214] When war was breaking out with Rome, Cleopatra decides to finance the war herself and is "determined to be there to oversee her investment."[215] No opposition is voiced from Antony, but he "reluctantly agreed" to this course of action.[216]

Cleopatra also has the upper hand in terms of decisions in the realm of politics. For instance, "she desired that he [Antony] should be forced to look to her alone for the fulfillment of his hopes."[217] Cleopatra's dominance over Antony can be demonstrated by the belief that "Cleopatra was moulding him to the shape of an eastern satrap."[218] It should not take one unaware then that J. Buchan reaches his premise that Antony is "wax in a woman's hands."[219] Antony has been prepared for his subservience to Cleopatra by his former marriage with Fulvia. Even though Hooper believes that Antony's submission to Cleopatra "may have been exaggerated by his [Antony's] enemies,"[220] truth remains at the heart of the matter. Antony is submissive to Cleopatra and the primary principles of the Isis cult are evident within their relationship. Cleopatra does enjoy authority over her husband for she is a living example of what Isis "gives" women the power to do: having power equal to that of men.

Isis also "compelled women to be loved by men" as evident from the Kyme Aretalogy. This principle is also manifest in Cleopatra's relationship with Antony. Cleopatra is truly loved by Antony and she becomes the "grand passion of his [Antony's] life."[221] Antony is also ready, willing, and able to sacrifice his own life for his wife if she can be spared after the tragic Battle of Actium.[222] While he sends a message to Octavian that demonstrates his resolve to carry out his plan, Octavian fails to issue a reply.[223] The willingness to lay down his own life suggests that Antony considers his wife more significant than himself. Is this noble act due to his great love for Cleopatra as his wife or deference to her power as queen—an embodiment of the tenets of the Isis cult? Probably, the two cannot be separated.

The control that Cleopatra has over Antony are symptomatic of a greater dilemma: the epidemic of the Isis cult. As queen, Cleopatra's endorsement of the Isis cult stands only to enhance its influence among her people. The profound effect of Isiac devotion in Egypt, not surprisingly, affects such critical aspects of Egyptian life that have been detailed, such as the relationships of the Isis cult being imitated by the Ptolemaic dynasty.

CONCLUSION

In conclusion, the origin of Isis has been traced from three primary documents as written by Plutarch, Apuleius, and Diodorus. Contrasts, comparisons, and historical accuracy have been focused upon concerning the accounts of these primary documents in order to critically assess the continuity and occasional discrepancies among them. Using these documents as a starting point, the scope of influence that Isis supposedly exercises has been examined. Isis demonstrates her influence in a number of areas, such as law-making, fate, creation, magic, healing, salvation, gender roles, and so forth. Some of the areas over which Isis exerts her influence also parallel Christian ideas. Similarities can be characterized in creation roles, calling upon a deity as a source of help, and salvation being granted to devotees. Since Isis is an Egyptian goddess, attention has also been given to her influence in Egyptian society. Isis leaves her imprint upon Egyptian society before traveling into the Greco-Roman empire. By understanding these roots of the Isis cult in Egypt, a greater appreciation will ensue as this cult is studied in Greco-Roman society.

NOTES

1. Geb is an alternate spelling for Seb.
2. Introduction to Plut., *De Is. et Os.* (Babbitt, LCL), 3.
3. D. A. R., "Plutarch," *OCD*, 1200.
4. Introduction to Plut., *De Is. et Os.* (Babbitt, LCL), 3.
5. Introduction to Plut., *De Is. et Os.* (Babbitt, LCL), 4. Cf. G. Nagel, "The 'Mysteries' of Osiris in Ancient Egypt," in *The Mysteries: Papers from the Eranos Yearbooks* (Bollingen Series; 30 vols.; vol. 2 of *Papers from the Eranos Yearbooks*, ed. J. Campbell, trans. R. Manheim and R. F. C. Hull; Princeton: Princeton University Press, 1955), 119; I. Shaw and P. Nicholson, "Osiris" *DAE*, 214.
6. A. Tripolitis, *Religions of the Hellenistic-Roman Age* (Grand Rapids: Eerdmans, 2002), 26.
7. Shaw and Nicholson, "Osiris," *DAE*, 214.
8. Sir W. Budge, *Egyptian Religion* (New York: Bell Publishing Company, 1959), 62.
9. Note that this version and all subsequent accounts have been condensed from the original versions.
10. Sir W. Budge, *Osiris and the Egyptian Resurrection* (2 vols.; London: Medici Society, 1911), 1:2.
11. These days come into being because the Sun gets angered by Rhea's sexual relations with Cronus, and lays a curse upon her. The result of this curse prohibits Rhea from giving birth during "any month or any year" (Plut., *De Is. et Os.* 355 d; Babbitt, LCL). However, Hermes delivers Rhea from this misfortune. He wins when he plays checkers with the moon and is awarded light, with a cumulative total of five days. These days become known as the birthdays of the gods.
12. Plut., *De Is. et Os.* 356 a-b (Babbitt, LCL). Nagel designates "king of the earth" as the primary role of Osiris in comparison with other attributes, such as the god of vegetation and the flood (Nagel, "The 'Mysteries' of Osiris in Ancient Egypt," 119).
13. Plut., *De Is. et Os.* 356 a-b (Babbitt, LCL).
14. Plut., *De Is. et Os.* 356 e (Babbitt, LCL).
15. Plut., *De Is. et Os.* 356 f (Babbitt, LCL). Diodorus Siculus writes that Anubis is the bodyguard of Osiris and Isis. Anubis, who is portrayed with the head of a dog protects Isis in her search for Osiris which is why he is honored during the Festival of Isis, for the "procession is led by dogs" (Dio. Sic., *Library of History* 1.87.3; Hanson, LCL).
16. Plut., *De Is. et Os.* 357 d (Babbitt, LCL).
17. The multitude of funerals by Isis for his various parts explains why so many tombs of Osiris exist in Egypt. Others believe that "she caused effigies of him to be made" which she presents to different cities as the body of Osiris (Plut., *De Is. et Os.* 358 b; Babbitt, LCL). In this fashion, she secures the honor for her husband and also does this as a safety precaution so Typhon would be at a loss to find the official tomb of Osiris.
18. This festival described here is probably known as the Pamylia Festival, held in honor of Osiris, where a triple statue of his phallus is presented. The significance

of this is to recognize Osiris as "the Source, and every source, by its fecundity, multiplies what proceeds from it" (Plut., *De Is. et Os.* 365 b; Babbitt, LCL). The impact of the Osiris-Isis myth upon Egyptian society can be deemed successful because people take the ideas in the pagan myths and assimilate them into their culture, revealing the influence that such stories had upon society at large.

19. C. J. Bleeker, "Isis as Saviour Goddess," in *The Saviour God: Comparative Studies in the Concept of Salvation* (ed. S. G. F. Brandon; Manchester: Manchester University Press, 1963), 6.

20. Bleeker, "Saviour Goddess," 6.

21. R. J. Getty, "Isis," *OCD*, 768.

22. *Metamorphoses* is known later as "The Golden Ass."

23. Witt speaks for the majority when he comments, "From the pages of Apuleius we can gain much invaluable knowledge of the main features of Isiac initiation as it was practised in the imperial age" (*Isis in the Ancient World*, 158), which explains why scholars use *Metamorphoses* as their historical basis for Isiac initiation.

24. E. Fantham, *Roman Literary Culture: From Cicero to Apuleius* (Baltimore: Johns Hopkins University Press, 1996), 262.

25. Introduction to Apul., *Metam.*, page xii (Hanson, LCL). The author of this account, Apuleius, is born in approximately AD 125. He might be compared to Eusebius (author of *Ecclesiastical History*), in that he writes of history which precedes his time period. In other words, the historicity of the account should not be deemed problematic because of his birth in the early second century.

26. Apul., *Metam.* 11.3. The border of this cloak hangs in the form of a "special knot between the breasts that was a distinctive feature of Isiac dress" (footnote 1, 296; Hanson, LCL). This Isiac knot is a factual tidbit incorporated into the account (Witt, *Isis in the Ancient World*, 55; cf. M. D. Donalson, *The Cult of Isis in the Roman Empire: Isis Invicta*; Studies in Classics 22; Lewiston: Edwin Mellen Press, 2003, 101).

27. Apul., *Metam.* 11.4 (Hanson, LCL). Perhaps the flowers might be linked to the wreath of roses that Lucius eats which begins his transformation.

28. Apul., *Metam.* 11.5 (Hanson, LCL).

29. Apul., *Metam.* 11.5 (Hanson, LCL).

30. Apul., *Metam.* 11.5 (Hanson, LCL). Notice the longevity of this holiday (also known as the *Navigium Isidis*) which marks the beginning of the season of navigation.

31. Apul., *Metam.* 11.5 (Hanson, LCL).

32. Apul., *Metam.* 11.6 (Hanson, LCL). The sistrum, used by Isis's priest in this instance is "pertinent to the cult" of Isis (R. A. Wild, *Water in the Cultic Worship of Isis and Sarapis*; Leiden: E. J. Brill, 1981, 45).

33. Apul., *Metam.* 11.6 (Hanson, LCL). Isis may express her distaste of the animal form of Lucius because the donkey may have been "associated with Seth," the murderer of Osiris (Hanson, 302, footnote 1; LCL).

34. Hanson comments that perhaps Lucius fears that he will be charged as a magician, which is a "serious offence in Roman law" (302, footnote 2; LCL).

35. Apul., *Metam.* 11.6 (Hanson, LCL).

36. Apul., *Metam.* 11.6 (Hanson, LCL).

37. Apul., *Metam.* 11.6 (Hanson, LCL). Notice that Isis supposedly exhibits power over the fate of individuals, such as Lucius.

38. Apul., *Metam.* 11.7 (Hanson, LCL).

39. Apul., *Metam.* 11.9 (Hanson, LCL).

40. Apul., *Metam.* 11.9 (Hanson, LCL).

41. Apul., *Metam.* 11.9 (Hanson, LCL). According to *P. Oxy. XI.1380*, Isis is the "lady of light and flames."

42. Apul., *Metam.* 11.9 (Hanson, LCL). The "Greater Vows" are also probably better known as prayers uttered to Isis as recorded in Apul., *Metam.* 11.17 (Hanson, 308, footnote 2; LCL).

43. Sarapis is a Hellenized god and has been described as the fusion of Apis (an Egyptian bull whose mother is Isis) and Osiris (Jordan, "Sarapis," *Encyclopedia of Gods*, 228).

44. Apul., *Metam.* 11.10 (Hanson, LCL). Note that this shrill sound appears to correlate with the sound that Isis and Nephthys make when mourning over Osiris. These two goddesses are "often identified with birds," such as the kite, which is thought to "possess the same pitch as the shrill sound of the ancient Egyptian lamentation" (Bleeker, "*Saviour Goddess*," 8). In terms of the account by Apuleius, the shrill sound by the initiates corresponds to the Isis cult and the historical relevancy bolsters the authenticity of the account.

45. Apul., *Metam.* 11.10 (Hanson, LCL).

46. Apul., *Metam.* 11.10 (Hanson, LCL). The golden boat is fitting for the commencement of the season of navigation.

47. Apul., *Metam.* 11.10 (Hanson, LCL).

48. Apul., *Metam.* 11.10 (Hanson, LCL). These objects carried by the priests are representative of Isis in one form or another. For example, Hanson comments that Anubis "shared characteristics of Mercury" (310, footnote 1; Hanson, LCL). The references to the breast and milk also may also describe Isis as mother, for many pictures of Isis show her suckling her son Horus. Isis is also referenced as a "beautiful animal [or a cow] of all the gods" in *P. Oxy XI.1380* (Kraemer's brackets).

49. Apul., *Metam.* 11.11 (Hanson, LCL). The mother of all is indicative of Isis.

50. Apul., *Metam.* 11.11 (Hanson, LCL).

51. Apul., *Metam.* 11.12 (Hanson, LCL).

52. Apul., *Metam.* 11.12 (Hanson, LCL).

53. Apul., *Metam.* 11.16 (Hanson, LCL).

54. Apul., *Metam.* 11.15 (Hanson, LCL).

55. Apul., *Metam.* 11.16 (Hanson, LCL), emphasis added. Note the Christian parallels with the language of being reborn and service to the deity.

56. Apul., *Metam.* 11.16 (Hanson, LCL).

57. Apul., *Metam.* 11.16 (Hanson, LCL).

58. Apul., *Metam.* 11.16 (Hanson, LCL). In myths surrounding Isis, grain is significant because the resurrection of grain is symbolic of Isis resurrecting Osiris. The milk, also, corresponds to Isis as a "mother goddess" (Jordan, "Isis," *Encyclopedia of Gods*, 118).

59. Apul., *Metam.* 11.17 (Hanson, LCL). The translation is suggested by Hanson, (342, footnote 1; LCL). *Pastophori* may also describe the bearers of the boat of Isis

(Donalson, *Cult of Isis*, 50).

60. Apul., *Metam.* 11.17. Donalson comments that "the *Navigium* festival significantly came to be connected specifically to the Roman imperial ideology," particularly because of the prayers offered here, which are "identified with the famous *vota*, vows for the safety and prosperity of the emperor and the empire as a whole" (*Cult of Isis*, 69). The prayers for those in authority also echo biblical references (1 Tim 2.1-2; Rom 13.1-4).

61. Isis is believed to protect the seas as evident from *P. Oxy. XI.1380*, for Isis is described as the "guardian and guide of seas, and Lady of the mouths and rivers" as well as from the Kyme Aretalogy, "I am the Queen of rivers and winds and sea . . . I stir up the sea and I calm it. . . I am the Queen of seamanship. I make the navigable unnavigable when it pleases me." The Kyme Aretalogy also credits Isis as the one initiating trade in the seas, for "I [Isis] devised business in the sea."

62. Apul., *Metam.* 11.19 (Hanson, LCL).

63. Apul., *Metam.* 11.19.

64. Apul., *Metam.* page 328, footnote 1 (Hanson, LCL).

65. Apul., *Metam.* 11.20 (Hanson, LCL).

66. Apul., *Metam.* 11.20 (Hanson, LCL).

67. Apul., *Metam.* 11.21 (Hanson, LCL).

68. Apul., *Metam.* 11.21 (Hanson, LCL).

69. Apul., *Metam.* 11.21 (Hanson, LCL).

70. Apul., *Metam.* 11.21 (Hanson, LCL).

71. Apul., *Metam.* 11.22 (Hanson, LCL).

72. The plural form is intended here.

73. Apul., *Metam.* 11.22 (Hanson, LCL).

74. The baths that Lucius describes here bear striking parallels to the Christian baptism, especially in the presence of "believers" and being part of the initiation process.

75. Apul., *Metam.* 11.23 (Hanson, LCL).

76. Apul., *Metam.* 11.23 (Hanson, LCL).

77. In his work, *The Lives of the Caesars*, Suetonius confirms the historicity of the linen robe as appropriate for Isiac initiates, for Otho would "celebrate the rites of Isis publicly in the linen garment prescribed by the cult" (Otho 12.1-2; Rolfe, LCL). On a contrasting note, H. C. Kee generalizes from his commentary on Plutarch's *De Is. et Os.* that "the true devotee of Isis is not known by the linen garment or shaved head, but by the exercise of reason and the study of philosophy in order to discern the truth within the mysteries revealed by her" (*Miracle in the Early Christian World: A Study in Sociohistorical Method*; New Haven: Yale University Press, 1983), 142.

78. Apul., *Metam.* 11.23 (Hanson, LCL).

79. Donalson, *Cult of Isis*, 30. Donalson offers the possibility of the experience of Lucius as an hallucination (30).

80. Apul., *Metam.* 11.23 (Hanson, LCL).

81. These twelve robes are symbolic, according to Witt, for they are representative of the "symbols of the twelve 'regions' or 'zones' through which he would have passed" (*Isis in the Ancient World*, 161).

82. Apul., *Metam.* 11.24 (Hanson, LCL).

83. Apul., *Metam.* 11.24 (Hanson, LCL).

84. Apul., *Metam.* 11.23 (Hanson, LCL). Willoughby believes that Lucius can now be seen as "a personification of the sun-god" with his "Olympian stole, his lighted torch, and his rayed crown" (*Pagan Regeneration*, 191). Although somewhat odd in nature, the actions that Lucius undergo can be classified as "a rite of deification" (Willoughby, *Pagan Regeneration*, 191) where he becomes "treated as Osiris-Ra" (Willoughby, *Pagan Regeneration*, 192).

85. Apul., *Metam.* 11.24 (Hanson, LCL).

86. Apul., *Metam.* 11.24 (Hanson, LCL).

87. Apul., *Metam.* 11.25 (Hanson, LCL).

88. Apul., *Metam.* 11.26 (Hanson, LCL).

89. Wild, *Water in the Cultic Worship*, 170, citing Hawthorne, *Archaeology* 18 (1965), 199; Handler, *AJA* 75 (1971), 62.

90. Donaldson, *Cult of Isis*, 38.

91. Diod. Sic., *Library of History* 1.11.1 (Oldfather, LCL).

92. Diod. Sic., *Library of History* 1.11.2.

93. Diod. Sic., *Library of History* 1.11.2 (Oldfather, LCL).

94. Diod. Sic., *Library of History* 1.11.4 (Oldfather, LCL). Witt also affirms the truth of Isis's ancient birth saying, "There, in the beginning was Isis. Oldest of the old, she was the goddess from whom all Becoming arose" (*Isis in the Ancient World*, 14).

95. Diod. Sic., *Library of History* 1.11.4. In the Egyptian mindset, Isis is portrayed as a cow. Furthermore, Apuleius records that a cow is carried in the Isiac procession (*Metam.* 11.11).

96. Diod. Sic., *Library of History* 1.11.5 (Oldfather, LCL).

97. Diod. Sic., *Library of History* 1.11.5 (Oldfather, LCL).

98. Diod. Sic., *Library of History* 1.11.5 (Oldfather, LCL).

99. Diod. Sic., *Library of History* 1.11.6 (Oldfather, LCL).

100. The discussion of other gods and goddesses continues in 1.12.3-10. Homer also believes that the gods visited the cities of men and observed their ways (*Od.* 17.485-87).

101. The addition of five days is a common thread that also exists in Plutarch's account (Plut., *De Is. et Os.* 355 d).

102. The character of Isis was "absorbed, or equated with, many other divinities, acquiring a universal character expressed in Gk. as μυριώνυμος, 'invoked by innumerable names'" (Getty, "Isis," *OCD*, 768, cf. Plut., *De Is. Et Os.* 372 e).

103. Plutarch also records that Osiris helped the Egyptians to become more civilized in the areas of agriculture, legislature, and devotion to pagan deities (Plut., *De Is. et Os.* 356 a-b).

104. Diod. Sic., *Library of History* 1.14.1 (Oldfather, LCL). The crown of Isis, as recorded by Apuleius, confirms the connection of Isis and wheat for the top of her crown is decorated with this grain (Apul., *Metam.* 11.3). Getty also notes that Isis was "guarantor of the fertility of fields and the abundance of harvests" ("Isis," 768).

105. Diod. Sic., *Library of History* 1.14.1 (Oldfather, LCL). Osiris is also seen as a vegetation god and associated with a grain god in Egypt named Neper. His attributes are "absorbed by Osiris" (Budge, *Egyptian Resurrection*, 1:58). Plutarch also clarifies Osiris as a fertility god. Osiris is also noted for being "the whole source and

faculty creative of moisture" which is thought to be the "cause of generation and the substance of life-producing seed" (Plut., *De Is. et Os.* 364 a; Babbitt, LCL).

106. Diod. Sic., *Library of History* 1.14.2 (Oldfather, LCL).

107. Diod. Sic., *Library of History* 1.14.2-3 (Oldfather, LCL). The idea of Isis being associated with the grain correlates with her role of causing the resurrection of Osiris as a fertility god. Isis is believed to give life to Osiris, thus causing germination (or the "resurrection") of the grain. See E. Stroubal, *Life of the Ancient Egyptians* (trans. D. Viney; Norman: University of Oklahoma Press, 1992), 96; R. Turcan, *The Cults of the Roman Empire* (trans. A. Nevill; Oxford: Blackwell, 1996), 118.

108. Diod. Sic., *Library of History* 1.14.3.

109. The Kyme Aretalogy also states that "I [Isis] am called the Lawgiver" and "established penalties for those who practice injustice."

110. Diod. Sic., *Library of History* 1.15.8 (Oldfather, LCL).

111. Diod. Sic., *Library of History* 1.17.1 (Oldfather, LCL).

112. Diod. Sic., *Library of History* 1.17.1-2 (Oldfather, LCL).

113. Diod. Sic., *Library of History* 1.17.3 (Oldfather, LCL). Osiris does not leave Isis without assistance for he provides Hermes as her counselor.

114. Diod. Sic., *Library of History* 1.20.3-4 (Oldfather, LCL).

115. Diod. Sic., *Library of History* 1.20.6 (Oldfather, LCL).

116. Diod. Sic., *Library of History* 1.22.6 (Oldfather, LCL).

117. The Greeks "honor this member" or "phallus" in the Osiris cult, including his rites and sacrifices (Diod. Sic., *Library of History* 1.22.7; Oldfather, LCL). In the account recorded by Plutarch, Isis honors Osiris's phallus in the "festival of the Pamylia" (Plut., *De Is. et Os.* 365 b; Babbit, LCL).

118. Diod. Sic., *Library of History* 1.21.5 (Oldfather, LCL).

119. Diod. Sic., *Library of History* 1.21.6 (Oldfather, LCL).

120. Diod. Sic., *Library of History* 1.22.2 (Oldfather, LCL). However, some believe that the bodies of Osiris and Isis are not in Memphis, but on an island in the Nile. On this island, the tomb of Osiris resides. The Egyptian priests pay homage to this tomb in their daily ritual: pouring milk into 360 bowls around his tomb while invoking the names of Isis and Osiris in song.

121. Diod. Sic., *Library of History* 1.25.5 (Oldfather, LCL).

122. The appointment of Horus as king is confirmed later in the account of Diodorus for Horus is the last ruling god (Diod. Sic., *Library of History* 1.44.1).

123. Note that the statements expressed here should be viewed from the standpoint of developing an Isiac theology. Isis is a mythological character and an examination of her character should be understood within these proper parameters.

124. *P. Oxy. XI.1380.*

125. S. K. Heyob, *The Cult of Isis Among Women in the Greco-Roman World* (E. J. Brill: Leiden, 1975), 113.

126. Diod. Sic., *Library of History* 1.27.2 (Oldfather, LCL).

127. Although there is not a direct antecedent of the term, sister, it can be logically deduced from the lines that follow, especially the seventh line as quoted here.

128. Lichtheim, *The New Kingdom*, 83.

129. Lichtheim, *The New Kingdom*, 81.

130. F. Solmsen, *Isis among the Greeks and Romans* (Marvin Classical Lectures 25; Cambridge: Harvard University Press, 1979), 44.

131. Donalson, *Cult of Isis*, 19.

132. Kyme Aretalogy.

133. Kyme Aretalogy.

134. Plut.'s *De Is. et Os.* (as condensed here) "contained just those elements which for later antiquity could serve as the pattern of family bonds of affection"(Witt, *Isis in the Ancient World*, 41).

135. Isis also does the unexpected in raising her husband's child, Anubis, from his sexual union with her sister.

136. Heyob, *Cult of Isis among Women*, 44. See also Witt for his praise of Isis as "faithful wife" and "model spouse" (*Isis in the Ancient World*, 41).

137. Kyme Aretalogy

138. Diod. Sic., *Library of History* 1.27.1-2.

139. Diod. Sic., *Library of History* 1.27.4 (Oldfather, LCL).

140. Kyme Aretalogy.

141. Witt, *Isis in the Ancient World*, 19.

142. *P. Oxy. XI.1380.*

143. Donalson, *Cult of Isis*, 1.

144. *P. Oxy. XI.1380.*

145. Kyme Aretalogy.

146. Kyme Aretalogy.

147. Kyme Aretalogy.

148. This is not necessarily to exclude other pagan deities who may have possessed control over the sea, however.

149. Kyme Aretalogy.

150. Apul., *Metam.* 11.4.

151. Apul., *Metam.* 11.10 (Hanson, LCL).

152. Apul, *Metam.* 11.9.

153. Diod. Sic., *Library of History* 1.12.2-3.

154. Diod. Sic., *Library of History* 1.11.1.

155. Kyme Aretalogy.

156. Kyme Aretalogy.

157. Witt, *Isis in the Ancient World*, 22; cf. Apul., *Metam.* 11.21.

158. L. R. LiDonnici, "Women's Religions and Religious Lives in the Greco-Roman City," in *Women and Christian Origins* (eds. R. S. Kraemer and M. R. D'Angelo; New York: Oxford University Press, 1999), 89.

159. LiDonnici, "Women's Religions," 89.

160. LiDonnici, "Women's Religions," 89.

161. LiDonnici, "Women's Religions," 89.

162. LiDonnici, "Women's Religions," 89-90.

163. LiDonnici, "Women's Religions, 90.

164. *P. Oxy. XI.1380.*

165. Witt, *Isis in the Ancient World*, 22.

166. G. Roeder, *Urkunden zur Religion des Alten Ägypten, Übersetzt und Eingeleitet* (Religiöse Stimmen der Völker; Jena: Eugen Diederichs, 1915), 90.

167. It should not be considered problematic that various myths are in existence concerning Isis. This is common in mythology, especially concerning Isis.

168. Witt, *Isis in the Ancient World*, 22.

169. Diod. Sic., *Library of History* 1.25.1.

170. Witt, *Isis in the Ancient World*, 22.

171. Diod. Sic., *Library of History* 1.25.5.

172. Witt, *Isis in the Ancient World*, 22

173. E. A. W. Budge, *An Introduction to Ancient Egyptian Literature* (Mineola: Dover Publications, 1997), 56.

174. Kee comments, "There is no figure in the study of religion in the ancient world — and perhaps in the entire scope of history and religion — whose role is more widespread in time and space and undergoes more marked transformation than that of Isis" (*Miracle in the Early Christian World*, 105).

175. Getty, "Isis," 768.

176. Diod. Sic., *Library of History* 1.13.5.

177. See Diod. Sic., *Library of History* 1.14.2-3

178. Nagle, *The Ancient World*, 50.

179. The Nile is paramount in Egypt for civilization to exist, especially agriculture. Even in modern culture, farmers are dependent upon the water of the Nile for the success of their crops.

180. Witt, *Isis in the Ancient World*, 14-5; cf. Donalson, *Cult of Isis*, 82.

181. *P. Oxy. XI.1380*.

182. This is not to overlook Osiris in the importance of the Nile, however. Every time that the river rises (which appears "dead"), Osiris is reborn as "the living water" (Witt, *Isis in the Ancient World*, 15). The death and birth of the river Nile symbolizes the concept of the resurrection which originates in Egyptian society.

183. Diod. Sic., *Library of History* 1.27.1-2 (Oldfather, LCL), emphasis added. Heyob examines evidence of marriage contracts in *Cult of Isis Among Women*, 43, footnote 29.

184. Since the Isis cult comes "into prominence in Egypt under the New Empire," approximately 1700-1100 BC (G. Showerman, "Isis," *ERE* 7:434), the Isis cult precedes the work by Sophocles (5th century BC) and the effects of the Isiac religion would have impacted society by this time.

185. Sophocles, *Oedipus at Colonus*, 337-41 (Storr, LCL).

186. L. Foreman, *Cleopatra's Palace: In Search of a Legend* (New York: Discovery Communications, 1999), 73.

187. Kee, *Miracle in the Early Christian World*, 117.

188. Kee, *Miracle in the Early Christian World*, 117.

189. Kee, *Miracle in the Early Christian World*, 117.

190. Kee, *Miracle in the Early Christian World*, 117. Ptolemy Philadelphus is also known as Ptolemy II.

191. Seti I is the son of King Ramses I and rules from 1291-1279 BC as an Egyptian king. He is also the second ruler of the nineteenth dynasty.

192. Lichtheim, *New Kingdom*, 56, under "C. The Decree" which is under the general category of "Dedication Inscriptions of Seti I" (52-57).

193. Lichtheim, *New Kingdom*, 56

194. Kee, *Early Christian World*, 117. Euergetes is also known as Ptolemy III.

195. Kee, *Early Christian World*, 117.

196. Kee, *Early Christian World*, 117. Philopator is also known as Ptolemy IV.

197. Foreman, *Cleopatra's Palace*, 71.

198. L. Hughes-Hallett, *Cleopatra: Histories, Dreams and Distortions* (New York: Harper & Row, 1990), 79.

199. Cleopatra will be recognized as simply "Cleopatra," but this is abbreviated for her official title as Cleopatra VII.

200. Hughes-Hallett, *Cleopatra: Histories*, 17.

201. Hughes-Hallett, *Cleopatra: Histories*, 19.

202. E. Bradford, *Cleopatra* (New York: Harcourt Brace Jovanovich, 1972), 13. This is not to mention the linguistic ability that Cleopatra possesses for she is well versed in multiple languages, or the courage she displays throughout her reign.

203. J. Lindsay (1st American ed.; New York: Coward McCann & Geoghegan, 1971), 293.

204. Hughes-Hallett, *Cleopatra: Histories*, 79.

205. Bradford, *Cleopatra*, 143.

206. Plut., *Ant.* 54.6 (Perrin, LCL).

207. Plut., *Ant.* 54.6 (Perrin, LCL).

208. Buchan, *Augustus*, 79.

209. Foreman, *Cleopatra's Palace*, 41.

210. Cassius Dio, *The Roman History: The Reign of Augustus* (trans. I. Scott-Kilvert; Harmondsworth: Penguin Books, 1987), 50.5. Hereafter, citation of Cassius Dio will be referenced as Dio Cassius, *Roman History*.

211. Dio Cassius, *Roman History*, page 262, footnote 18.

212. Dio Cassius, *Roman History*, 50.5.

213. D. L. Balch, *Let Wives Be Submissive: The Domestic Code in 1 Peter* (Society of Biblical Literature Monograph Series 26, eds. J. Crenshaw and R. Tannehill; Atlanta: Scholars Press, 1981), 71.

214. Hooper, *Roman Realities*, 306.

215. Hooper, *Roman Realities*, 306.

216. Hooper, *Roman Realities*, 306.

217. Buchan, *Augustus*, 102.

218. Buchan, *Augustus*, 103.

219. Buchan, *Augustus*, 102-103.

220. Hooper, *Roman Realities*, 307.

221. Foreman, *Cleopatra's Palace*, 150.

222. Foreman, *Cleopatra's Palace*, 150.

223. Foreman, *Cleopatra's Palace*, 150.

Chapter Two

Isis in the Greco-Roman World

This chapter will trace the development of the Isis cult in the Greco-Roman world. It will begin with Rome's initial opposition to the Isis cult and why it disapproves of this pagan religion. Namely, Rome opposes the goddess Isis because she is a threat to their constitution since Rome is established as a patriarchal society. Considerable attention will be paid to Augustus and his policies which lay the groundwork for the Roman empire. Also, tracing the responses of succeeding Roman emperors will document the eventual triumph of Isis from a persecuted cult to a powerful ally of the empire.

FROM CLEOPATRA (51-31 BC) TO AUGUSTUS (27 BC-AD 14)

Rome's Opposition to Cleopatra

Despite the fact that Cleopatra is well acclaimed in her native country, she is not popular with Rome. Rome is threatened by the success of Cleopatra, who is feared to jeopardize the position of Rome. J. Buchan writes, "That a woman and an eastern should presume to direct Roman armies and rule Roman lands cut Rome's pride to the quick. Moreover, there was a lurking dread of that spectre which had long haunted the western mind, domination by the East, and the transference of world-power from the Tiber to the Nile."[1] The true thoughts regarding Cleopatra are revealed clearly in the Battle of Actium. Dio Cassius records the words of Octavian addressing his soldiers,

> We Romans are the rulers of the greatest and best parts of the world, and yet we find ourselves spurned and trampled upon by a woman of Egypt. This disgraces our fathers. . . . It disgraces our own generation. . . . The men who achieved these feats of arms I have named would be cut to the heart if ever they knew that we

have been overcome by this pestilence of a woman. . . . They [the natives of Egypt and Alexandria] worship reptiles and beasts as gods, they embalm their bodies to make them appear immortal, they are most forward in effrontery, but most backward in courage. *Worst of all, they are not ruled by a man, but are the slaves of a woman.*[2]

The Romans believe that Cleopatra has manipulated Antony and essentially corrupted a Roman. Plutarch records that he "had been drugged and was not even master of himself."[3] Cleopatra is characterized as "the woman who had already ruined him and would make his ruin still more complete."[4] It is no surprise that the Roman soldiers resent Cleopatra in the battle with Octavian and the Roman citizens also dislike her.[5]

In addition to Cleopatra being a foreigner, Augustus (or Octavian) holds an unfavorable attitude toward her. Octavian's sister, Octavia, is originally married to Antony; however, Antony dismisses Octavia and her children from his house.[6] Antony divorces Octavia in 32 BC and marries Cleopatra.[7] This act may have been a contributing factor to the Battle of Actium on September 2, 31 BC. However, a power struggle between Antony and Augustus also escalates into this battle for dominance of the Roman world. Octavian is the victor in this battle. In the next year, 30 BC, Antony and Cleopatra commit suicide and Cleopatra's son, Caesarion, is executed in 30 BC by Octavian. Given the background of events, it is not surprising that Augustus would be opposed to the Isis cult, whose ideals Cleopatra represents.

Reasons for Opposition to Isis Cult by Rome

The Isiac religion is generally deemed problematic because it is "disruptive" to society.[8] The negative view of the Isis cult is largely because it is "foreign and suspicious"[9] and those involved in Egyptian cults (such as the Isis cult) are seen as "secret conspiratorial groups."[10] They are also viewed as siding with the government of Egypt in its conflicts with Rome. H. C. Kee explains, "As proponents of a religion which regarded rulers as hereditary representatives of the deity, their theory of kingship was in basic conflict with the conviction that the stability of the Roman state depended on perpetuation of the cult of the Roman gods."[11] Because of this conflict of interest, Augustus himself represses the Isis cult in a vigorous manner.[12] Isis is the supporter of Antony and Cleopatra which clashes against the Roman ancestral gods.[13] In Augustus's estimation, it is a wise political move to suppress the cult.

Augustus also attempts to forbid the Isis cult due to the possible immoral ramifications surrounding it. According to S. Pomeroy, Isis is "seductive" just as Cleopatra is.[14] In this light, the seductive nature of Isis may conflict with the morality that Augustus wishes to institute during his reign. It is believed that "the gods of Egypt threatened to undermine the new moral foundations of society which Augustus hoped to establish by legislation."[15]

Isis: A Threat to the Roman Constitution as a Patriarchal Society

The tenets of the Isis cult contradict that of the Roman constitution. Rome is founded by Romulus in 753 BC according to legend. Romulus is known as the first king of Rome[16] and comes to power in the fifth century BC.[17] In the *Roman Antiquities of Dionysius of Halicarnassus*, written in 37-30 BC, the foundation of laws is described: "Romulus also seems to have been the author of that good discipline in other matters by the observance of which the Romans have kept their commonwealth flourishing for many generations."[18] In other words, the establishment of laws served as the backbone for their country. To neglect to obey these laws may hinder the progress and development of the people of Rome.

Balch comments that in "Greek political writing and rhetoric, the discussion of the 'constitution' and of the 'household' were very closely related."[19] Dionysius avers that the success of Rome is dependent upon the Roman constitution being upheld in the lives of households. He writes that every

> state, since it consists of many families, is most likely to enjoy tranquility when the lives of the individual citizens are untroubled, and to have a *very tempestuous* time when the private affairs of the citizens are in a bad way, and that every prudent statesman, whether he be a lawgiver or a king, ought to introduce such laws as will make the citizens just and temperate in their lives.[20]

The state is responsible for introducing laws for its citizens that would enable them to live peaceful, harmonious lives. To not do so would be for the state to shirk its responsibilities.[21] As a means of accomplishing this, laws concerning marital relations, and the role of husbands and wives are issued. Balch writes, "Dionysius, too, observed in his rhetorical encomium that 'cities' are composed of many 'houses' (*Rom. Ant.* II.24.2), so that the constitution must regulate marriages (II.24.14) or the whole state will come to ruin."[22]

Rom. Ant. II.25.4-5 records that one of the laws

> obliged both the married women, as having no other refuge, to conform themselves entirely to the temper of their husbands, and the husbands to rule their wives as necessary and inseparable possessions. Accordingly, if a wife was virtuous and in all things obedient to her husband, she was mistress of the house to the same degree as her husband was master of it.[23]

These words alone are enough to document the opposition that Rome may have had to the Isis cult—a cult that "undoubtedly underlay and sustained the prominent position of women in Egyptian society."[24]

Rome is also established as a patriarchal society. Pomeroy details the reasoning behind this, saying, "The weakness and light-mindedness of the female sex (*infirmitas sexus* and *levitas animi*) were the underlying principles of Roman legal theory that mandated all women to be under the custody of males."[25]

Rome's patriarchal society is evident in the ancient laws concerning adultery. Dionysius writes in *Rom. Ant.* II.25.6.7 that

> other offences, however, were judged by her [the wife's] relations together with her husband; among them was adultery, or where it was found she had drunk wine—a thing which the Greeks would look upon as the least of all faults. For *Romulus permitted them to punish both these acts with death, as being the gravest offences women could be guilty of*, since he looked upon adultery as the source of reckless folly, and drunkenness as the source of adultery.[26]

Evidently, a Roman wife is not permitted to drink wine even though this fails to be an issue for Greeks. Both adultery and drunkenness are teamed as deserving of capital punishment which fosters the conclusion that Roman law concerning women might be classified as extreme.

These harsh laws are thought to be beneficial for women, as the following attests: "These, then, are the excellent laws which Romulus enacted concerning women, by which he rendered them more observant of propriety in relation to their husbands."[27] The demonstrative adjective "these" begs an explanation. Is this statement a reference to the entirety of the laws explained in section 25? It appears so. The laws as covered in section 25 are three-fold, but all these laws can be defined by one central concept: the behavior of wives. The first law "was to this effect, that a woman joined to her husband by a holy marriage should share in all his possessions and sacred rites."[28] The second law is recorded in *Rom. Ant.* II. 25.4-5 (above) and the third law is found in *Rom. Ant.* II. 25.6-7 (above).

From the modern mindset, classifying these laws as excellent may be rendered problematic, since such an explanation for the existence of some of the laws concerning women or wives, especially concerning drunkenness, are not logically grounded. They merely fall back on the assumed tradition that Romulus considers women to be more "observant of propriety."[29]

In the mindset of Dionysius, these laws are worthy of excellent status because of the results that they achieve. Because adultery and drinking wine by wives is punishable by death, divorce in Rome is nonexistent for 520 years, a substantial period of time.[30]

In conclusion, Rome may be predisposed against the Isis cult because it clashes with its founding principles as a patriarchal society. Roman wives are under the authority of their husbands, and the wives are ruled as possessions of their spouses. This would conflict with the liberation of women that the Isis cult endorses. However, the enemy of Rome—Cleopatra, who embodies the

Isis cult—does not help Rome view this cult in a favorable light either. The combination of these two elements should have been too much for the Isis cult to overcome, but it would prevail in the midst of persecution.

Power of the Paterfamilias

Another critical component of the foundation of Rome is the power of the *paterfamilias*. Pomeroy provides a clear overview of the *paterfamilias* in Roman history, as follows:

> In childhood, a daughter fell under the sway of the eldest male ascendant in her family, the *pater familias*. The power of the *pater familias* was without parallel in Greek law; it extended to the determination of life or death for all members of the household. Male offspring of any age were also subject to the authority of the *pater familias*, but as adults they were automatically emancipated upon his death, and the earliest Roman law code, the XII Tables (traditionally 451–450 B.C.) stated that a son who had been sold into slavery three times by his father thereby gained his freedom.[31]

Needless to say, the *paterfamilias* is limited to men. Women have no authority in this respect. J. A. C. Thomas explains the role of men concerning the *paterfamilias* in detail:

> The concept of subjection to a single person, then, dominated, the concept of the family and could be applied to persons and things alike. Every man—women had no legal standing in this respect . . . either had power or was in power, i.e. was a *pater* or was *in potestate*; and the broad concept of *familia* explains why a male *sui iuris* was rightly styled a *paterfamilias* whether over the age of puberty or not—he was in his own *potestas* and that sufficed.[32]

The power as designated by the *paterfamilias* is rather extreme. In Roman society, the *paterfamilias* has power over the household and the affairs conducted in it. Dionysius records the laws surrounding the *paterfamilias* in *Roman Antiquities*. Essentially the *paterfamilias* has full control over his son for the duration of his life. This sphere of authority can be exercised through the following methods: imprisonment, physical labor in the fields (while in chains), and scourging.[33] These types of treatment can be extended to the son regardless of the power or position he may hold.[34]

The *paterfamilias* holds the power of life and death over his children and may punish them physically if desired.[35] Even if a son enters the political arena, he is not spared from the fear of the *paterfamilias*, but the threat of his father's power can actually become greater. Dionysius comments that because of the power of the *paterfamilias*, a son who has entered the political arena who may be delivering speeches from the platform of the speaker, or rostra, and enjoying the favor of the people, can be yanked from his rostra to endure harsh treatment from his father. Perhaps the father finds the words of his son unsuitable to his own ear or to those in the governmental body. The other authoritative personnel (such as the consul or tribune) hold no jurisdiction over the son to "rescue" him.[36]

Dionysius continues to elaborate on the rights of the *paterfamilias* and the nature of this power structure. He writes that according to Roman law,

> He [the Roman lawgiver] even allowed him [the father] to sell his son, without concerning himself whether this permission might be regarded as cruel and harsher than was compatible with natural affection. And, — a thing which anyone who has been educated in the lax manners of the Greeks may wonder at above all things and look upon as harsh and tyrannical, — he even gave leave to the father to make a profit by selling his son as often as three times, thereby *giving greater power to the father over his son than to the master over his slaves.*[37]

For this reason, the *paterfamilias* holds dominance over the members of the household with the sons being particularly highlighted in the history as recorded by Dionysius. In a sense, sons are essentially viewed as property as evident by their ability to be sold for money.

On a more positive note, emancipation from the *paterfamilias* is a possible reality and generally a positive event. A. Borkowski writes,

> Emancipation was normally used as a sensible family arrangement where a child was of mature years and in need of legal independence. Such an emancipation would be amicable: the child would be provided with a sizeable *peculium* [property], if possible, and would be made an heir or legatee in the will of the *paterfamilias.*[38]

However, not all emancipations go smoothly. A worst case scenario for one seeking emancipation involves being cast out of the house (or onto the streets) without the guarantee of *peculium*.[39] The *paterfamilias* can threaten the children in this manner or use this course of action as an act of punishment.[40]

AUGUSTUS: FIRST ROMAN EMPEROR

Considerable time and attention will be given to Augustus since he is the first Roman emperor. The decisions, rules, and legislation he establishes overshadow the work of his predecessors. In order to understand the founding of the Roman empire, it is critical to gain a solid appreciation and understanding of Augustus. Augustus sets the standard for the rest of the Roman emperors to follow. He is credited with reestablishing peace and unity after a series of civil wars. With this accomplishment, he is viewed as an authoritative figure and his ideas practiced long after his death.[41]

Popularity of Augustus

Augustus is a man revered long after his years. Because of the accomplishments of Augustus, he is "a god on earth" for many people since "only a supra-human being could have brought stability out of chaos."[42] D. Shotter writes, "Augustus was formally deified on 17 September, AD 14; but, for many, long before that date, he was the almost divine restorer upon whom the security of the whole edifice ultimately depended."[43] Augustus earns a positive reputation among the Romans for restoring order to society. For this reason, he is respected long after his time and has numerous implications for future Roman emperors.

Re-Instituting the Past

Augustus is a man who might be characterized by finding security in the principles of the past. Whether this be revitalizing "traditional religious practice" or emphasizing "old-fashioned family values,"[44] an elevated view of the past may be a trademark of Augustus. C. Freeman writes, "He [Augustus] was conservative by instinct, a reflection of both his temperament and his upbringing in a small provincial town outside Rome."[45] This taste of the past may have been transferred to the policies which are implemented during his reign. Augustus's personal preference is carried over into public practice in the areas of clothing and Roman customs, religion, and marriage, as noted by table 2.1 below.

While the measures passed by Augustus concerning clothing, Roman customs, and religion have mixed results, the only measure known to stand the test of time is the example set by Augustus concerning marriage. Augustus uses his power to recall the principles of the past in order to make them a present reality. In contrast to Egyptian history, which suggests that the roles of husband and wife are reversed because of the Isis cult, the role of male dominance over women in Roman history is foundational for Roman society as evident in the tenets of the Roman constitution.

Concerning Roman customs and clothing, Augustus's cherished notion of the past is evident by his disposition for family customs which is birthed in the confines of his home before this preference is extended into the public arena. Concerning his family, A. H. M. Jones writes, "He [Augustus] made the women of this family spin and weave in the old-fashioned way, and

Table 2.1. Augustus's Personal Preferences Becoming Public Practice

Issue	Augustus's Personal Preference	Public Practice	Historical Figure/ Authoritative Source	Results
Roman Customs/ Clothing	Augustus prefers the adornment of ancient togas.	Augustus requires people to wear togas to the Forum and its neighborhood.	Virgil, who says, "Romans, lord of the world, the toga-clad race."[46]	Questionable: Roman public officers are told to enforce the attire of togas to the Forum and its neighborhood.
Religion	Old religious ceremonies and cults are favored by Augustus.	Augustus requires people to wear togas to the Forum and its neighborhood.	Cleopatra, the hated enemy of Rome, is the personification of the Egyptian goddess Isis.	Limited: Hindering the spread of Isis in the Roman empire is futile.
Marriage	Augustus: "You yourselves ought to admonish and command your wives as you wish; that is what I do" as spoken to the senate in 19 BC.[47]	Augustus urges his senate to follow his example.	1) Metellus Macedonicus, who makes a speech calling wives an "annoyance."[48] 2) Probably Romulus, who issues a law that the husbands "rule their wives as necessary and inseparable possessions."[49]	Successful: Rome is encouraged and is upheld as a patriarchal society.

actually wore the homespun that they produced."[50] However, he attempts to extend his old-fashioned tastes to the general public as well. Jones comments, "He [Augustus] tried to make people wear the antiquated toga, which had gone out except for formal occasions."[51] In fact, Augustus takes this a step further and actually enforced the attire of togas at specific places. For instance, Augustus commanded the "aediles [Roman public officers] never again to allow anyone to appear in the Forum or its neighbourhood except in the toga and without a cloak."[52] Augustus makes his personal preferences practice for the Roman empire.

Augustus's favor of the past also affects religion. He "revived old ceremonies and offices and cults, and banned new foreign gods from the city."[53] The foreign gods would have included Isis, which is evidenced by the legislation banning Isis worship. This ban is politically motivated, "being intended to buttress the restored Republic."[54] However, securing his political agenda is not the only reason for his choices concerning religion. Rather, "there can be little doubt that Augustus valued them [ancient Roman customs and manners] for their own sake."[55]

Augustus's fixation on the past is also evident in his position on marriage. Augustus finds wives to be a necessary yet burdensome part of a man's life, agreeing with the view of Q. Caecilius Metellus Macedonicus. Metellus Macedonicus makes a speech describing wives to men as follows: "If we could get on without a wife, Romans, we would all avoid that annoyance; but since nature has ordained that we neither can live very comfortably with them nor at all without them, we must take thought for our lasting well-being rather than for the pleasure of the moment."[56] Essentially, Macedonicus is saying that "marriage and child-bearing, though unpleasant and irksome" are "necessary to the well-being of the state."[57] Augustus appears to capitalize upon this view in later history. In 19 BC, Augustus speaks to the senate: "You yourselves ought to admonish and command your wives as you wish; that is what I do."[58] In referring to Metellus Macedonicus, an authoritative figure from the past, to justify his own position on wives, Augustus continues to cement the foundation for Rome as a patriarchal society.

Augustus believes he is improving society by opposing change in the areas of clothing, Roman customs, marriage, and religion. The words of Augustus reflect the views of Cato.[59] As Jones writes, "Augustus was probably expressing real political sentiments when he said (of Cato)"[60] the following: "To seek to keep the established constitution unchanged argues a good citizen and a good man."[61] By retaining past Roman customs about marriage and religion, perhaps Augustus is attempting to stabilize the political order as well as being true to his citizenship.

Cato: Concerning Women and Wives

Because Augustus is influenced by Cato, it is critical to understand who Cato is and the ideas that he supports.[62] To what degree Cato is responsible for forming the mindset of Augustus on the demeanor of wives is uncertain, but Augustus does follow in his footsteps.

In order to fully understand this fact, it is necessary to examine the Oppian law in 215 BC which is issued by Rome because of a threat presented by Hannibal's army.[63] This law is "meant to be a temporary law that limited women's (but not men's), consumption of expensive goods."[64] The practice of the law stands so that even "twenty years later the danger had long passed but the law remained."[65] The confusion concerning this law escalates until 195 BC when "the women of Rome publicly demonstrated for its repeal" and "a public debate about the law" came into being.[66]

The full account of this incident in history has been recorded by Livy (59 BC-AD 17).[67] The debate centers around the " 'traditional' behavior of

women."[68] Cato, being conservative, argues "for the retention of the law."[69]
His argument is based on the following ideas, according to S. Young:

> women must be controlled, should have no voice in government, and if they
> repeal this law, it will only encourage women to interfere with other laws. He
> calls on the authority of the past, stating that Roman women have never acted
> on their own behalf, thus, *they had never been persons in the legal sense which
> was true in Roman law.*[70]

The words of Cato have been preserved by Livy. Cato speaks as follows:

> If they [the wives] win in this [the repeal of the Oppian law], what will they
> not attempt? Review all the laws with which your forefathers restrained their
> licence and made them subject to their husbands; even with all these bonds you
> can scarcely control them. What of this? If you suffer them to seize these bonds
> one by one and wrench themselves free and finally to be placed on a parity with
> their husbands, do you think that you will be able to endure them? The moment
> they begin to be your equals, they will be your superiors.[71]

Therefore, Cato thinks it would be best for husbands to retain strict authority
over their wives as the best means to keep women under control. He seems
to fear the cultural rise of women and considers it important to suppress this.
The view of women that governs the actions of Augustus runs parallel to what
is expressed by Cato.

Rewards and Penalties Supporting a Patriarchal Society

To promote his goal of populating the Roman empire, Augustus "increased
the rewards given to those who had children, and for the rest he introduced a
distinction between the married men and the unmarried by imposing different penalties on them."[72] However, some of the regulations as established by
Augustus favor men over women. Compared to her future husband the prospective bride has limited control in refusing the match. Pomeroy comments,
"The consent of both partners was necessary for the betrothal and marriage,
but the bride was allowed to refuse only if she could prove that the proposed
husband was morally unfit."[73]

Couples are given benefits if they have children. Women are penalized if
they choose not to conform to the plan of Augustus in procreation. Pomeroy
writes, "Under the Augustan marriage legislation, childlessness reduced the
amount [of property] that could be inherited, while motherhood increased
it."[74] Furthermore, in regard to the "right of three or four children," also
known as *ius liberorum*, "a freeborn woman who bore three children and
a freedwoman who bore four children were exempt from guardianship."[75]

However, even this exemption does not have the results that Augustus desires since it fails to "act as much of an incentive."[76] One thing is certain, however: Measures like these let women know that their role in Roman society is as mothers.

Augustus: Let No Woman Be Equal to Man

Augustus combats the principle of let no women be equal to a man in his speeches, laws, and actions. The words that Augustus speaks at the Battle of Actium are a good representation of his attitude toward women. He exhorts his soldiers, saying,

> I cannot describe to you any greater prize than that of upholding the renown which your forefathers won, of preserving the proud tradition of your native land, of punishing those who have rebelled against us, of conquering and ruling over all mankind, and *of allowing no woman to make herself equal to a man.*"[77]

Balch interprets this speech as "a stress on the 'customs of the fathers' with opposition to the Isis cult of Egypt and with the assertion that the 'new Isis' [or Cleopatra] reverses the proper relationship between man and woman."[78] The Battle of Actium is a battle between the Egyptian gods and the noble Roman gods. Augustus accuses Antony of being at war with the Roman gods besides being at war with Rome.[79]

Laws that are issued by Augustus also reveal a double standard. For instance, "Augustus declared adultery a public offense only in women."[80] This alone attests to the inequality between men and women in the mind of Augustus. If the wife does commit adultery, "the husband was obliged to divorce his wife," and a resulting trial would ensue.[81] Furthermore, "Penalties were laid down, too, for men who knowingly married women convicted of adultery or failing to divorce adulterous wives."[82] This same principle did not apply to the husband if he commits adultery. Almost two centuries later, the Roman jurist Ulpian (AD 193-213) finds the rules issued by Augustus to be unwarranted,[83] saying, "It is very unjust for a husband to require from a wife a level of morality that he does not himself achieve."[84] So, Augustus's legislation regarding women and adultery is later viewed by a few as extreme.

Inequality of women is not just limited to the adultery laws. Rather, it extends into other areas of legislation as well, such as criminal fornication (*stuprum*).[85] "No man was allowed to have sexual relations with an unmarried or widowed upper-class woman, but he could have relations with prostitutes, whereas upper-class women were not allowed to have any relations outside of marriage."[86] Evidently Augustus enforces these laws, even among the members of his family since he is known to have exiled his daughter and granddaughter for improper sexual relations and for canceling their right to be buried in his tomb.[87]

OFFICIAL ROMAN RESPONSES TO ISIS

Augustus

The power of Isis in Egyptian society is a threat to the power of Augustus in Rome. As a new Roman emperor, it is critical that he would establish himself in a credible fashion. In order to better understand this potential power struggle, table 2.2 has been utilized.

As table 2.2 illustrates, Isis can be classified as a rival for the power of Augustus in the areas of laws, government, and societal norms regarding women. For these reasons, Augustus decides to hinder the spread of the Isiac religion. To oppose the dangerous spread of the Isiac religion, Augustus issues laws against it. In 28 BC, Augustus forbids the worship of Egyptian gods within the *pomoerium* of the city of Rome.[89] The *pomoerium* can be described as "a strip of unoccupied sacred land which separated the area of civil and military jurisdiction."[90] Thus, "There were to be no new constructions [or "Isis rites"] in the sacred limits of Rome."[91] However, this does not affect practices of the Isis cult outside of the "city limits" of Rome, such as the Campus Martius.[92] This decree is not as successful as Augustus desires. When Agrippa, a Roman general and

Table 2.2. Comparison of Power Between Isis and Augustus

Power of Isis in Egyptian Society	*Power of Augustus in Rome*
Isis as "Lawgiver"	Augustus as lawgiver
Laws absolute: no man can make void her laws	Augustus establishes laws for the Roman empire
Isis "broke down the government of tyrants"[38]	Augustus is the authoritative one in power in the Roman empire
A law is established in Egyptian society for men to be allowed to marry their sisters	No such law is established (or even supported) in Roman society
Isis devises marriage contracts	Marriage laws are established by Augustus in 18 BC
Queen is given more honor and power than king	King is in control and has more power than queen
Husbands agree to be obedient to wives	Wives are under the control of their husbands
Woman are equal to men	Women are not equal to men according to Augustus; consider also the power of the *paterfamilias*

statesman (63-12 BC), finds that the worship of Egyptian gods "had revived, strengthened the ban and extended it for one mile beyond the *pomoerium*."[93]

Despite the legislation to hamper the Isiac religion, its spread could not be stopped. One reason for its growth was because of the makeup of the population of Rome. Jones writes, "The immigrants, slave and free, who formed a large percentage of the population [of Rome], naturally tended to cling to the gods of their various homelands. Some of these, like Serapis and Isis, attracted indigenous Romans."[94] The diversity of religion infiltrates with the Roman masses which results in people straying from the Roman gods to embrace others such as Isis.

Kee also speaks of the ineffectiveness of the efforts to ban Isis. He says, "So great was the appeal of beneficent Isis to the Roman populace that the attempt to suppress her cult on political grounds was a failure."[95] Kee also notes the utter devotion of Isis enthusiasts, saying, "Her devotees would accept martyrdom rather than abandon her worship."[96] Pomeroy writes that the cult of Isis "competed too successfully with the imperial revival of traditional Roman religion. Isis was too popular to suppress."[97] Thus, the appeal of devotion to Isis is so strong that limiting legislation and even persecution does nothing but fuel the flames of its growth throughout the empire.

Other Roman Emperors

Augustus is not the only emperor opposed to the Isiac religion. He is later joined by the Emperor Tiberius (AD 14-37). Tiberius issues a time of "repression" for the Isis devotees "due to a scandal in a temple of Isis."[98] However, after this period, Isis grows in favor with the Roman emperors. A. Roullet records that the "Isiac religion settled permanently in Rome with the approval and participation of most of the Emperors."[99] Isis takes root in Rome and its influence permeates the Roman provinces. Furthermore, "the harbour of Rome, as all Mediterranean ports, was a centre for the Isiac cults."[100]

Caligula (AD 37-41), the successor of Tiberius, rebuilds a temple to Isis known as the Isis Campense in the Campus Martius.[101] Pomeroy suggests that Caligula is the first emperor "to take advantage of the popularity that might accrue to an emperor who favored Isis."[102] The construction of the Isis Campense is a sizeable accomplishment in terms of the Isis cult since it is "the greatest of the Roman Iseums."[103]

The following emperor, Claudius, also accepts the Isiac religion. Roullet writes, "The cartouche of Claudius (41-54) was inlaid on the Mensa Isiaca."[104] In other words, a resemblance of Claudius is set on the surface of this altar top. The *Mensa Isiaca* is also known as the "Bembine Table of Isis"[105] and is actually "the top of a Roman altar to Isis."[106] The *Mensa Isica* is also detailed by "mystical symbols and figures."[107]

Nero (AD 54-68), the emperor after Claudius, recognizes Isis as a goddess for he includes "Isiac festivals on the Roman calendar."[108] Under his reign the role of Isis continues to grow. The endorsement of Isis continues from later emperors. Vespasian (AD 69-79) demonstrates his regard for Isis by visiting the Serapeum in Alexandria[109] and by issuing coins representative of the Isis temple in Rome. Titus, the next emperor (AD 79-81), pays his respects to Isis by visiting a Serapeum in Memphis and even officiates at the "burial or installation of an Apis."[110] Apis is significant in terms of Isis because Isis is known as "Mother of the Apis bull."[111] Assisting with the ceremony indicates the acceptance of Isiac religion. Titus also gives credit for his victory in the Judaean war by spending the night at the Iseum Campense.[112]

The next emperor, Domitian (AD 81-96), rebuilds the Iseum Campense which is destroyed by fire in AD 80 under the reign of Titus.[113] Roullet comments, Domitian "owed his life to the priests of Isis" which contributes to his rebuilding the Iseum Campense.[114] Roullet also credits Domitian for the Iseum of Beneventum which was "probably built in his reign."[115]

In summary, while Isis is originally opposed by Augustus and Tiberius, its reception by succeeding Roman emperors is favorable, especially as it begins to flourish in Rome itself. By building the Iseum Campense in the Campus Martius, Rome sets a precedent for the rest of the provinces.

CONCLUSION

This chapter has attempted to prove that the Isis cult began as a threat to patriarchal Roman society. The laws issued by Augustus evidence the inequality that existed between men and women in that time. Since Isis is seen as the emancipator of women, this posed a problem. Augustus may have felt that the "power" of Isis was a threat to his rule as emperor. However, despite the persecution of Isis devotees, the Isis cult continued to flourish. In time, the Isis cult could not be suppressed by legislation. Later emperors embrace the Isis cult, increasing its popularity at the time when Christianity would begin its march across the empire.

NOTES

1. Buchan, *Augustus*, 105.
2. Dio Cassius, *Roman History* 50.24 (Scott-Kilvert), emphasis added.
3. Plut., *Ant.* 60.1 (Perrin, LCL).
4. Plut., *Ant.* 66.5 (Perrin, LCL).

5. Hooper, *Roman Realities*, 306. The hatred by the Romans may also have been accentuated since Cleopatra is not a Roman citizen. (Romans hold a particular dislike towards foreigners and trust wanes toward those who are not of Roman blood.)

6. Hooper, *Roman Realities*, 306.

7. The marriage of Antony to Cleopatra may have also fueled Augustus's distaste for Cleopatra.

8. M. Y. MacDonald, "Rereading Paul: Early Interpreters of Paul on Women and Gender," in *Women and Christian Origins* (eds. Kraemer and D'Angelo), 243.

9. MacDonald, "Rereading Paul," 243.

10. Kee, *Miracle in the Early Christian World*, 129.

11. Kee, *Miracle in the Early Christian World*, 129.

12. C. Bailey, *Phases in the Religion of Ancient Rome* (Westport: Greenwood Press, 1972), 186.

13. Bailey, *Religion of Ancient Rome*, 186.

14. S. B. Pomeroy, *Goddesses, Whores, Wives, and Slaves: Women in Classical Antiquity* (New York: Schocken Books, 1995), 224.

15. Pomeroy, *Women in Classical Antiquity*, 224. The legislation that Augustus issued will be discussed later.

16. J. A. C. Thomas, *Textbook of Roman Law* (Amsterdam: North-Holland Publishing Company, 1976), 13.

17. However, in some variations of this legend, Romulus's brother, Remus, also shares in this accomplishment.

18. Dionysius of Halicarnassus, *Rom. Ant.* II.24.1 (Cary, LCL).

19. Balch, *Wives*, 55.

20. Dionysius of Halicarnassus, *Rom. Ant.* II.24.2-3 (Cary, LCL), emphasis added.

21. Dionysius of Halicarnassus, *Rom. Ant.* II.24.2.

22. Balch, *Wives*, 55.

23. Dionysius of Halicarnassus, *Rom. Ant.* II.25.4-5 (Cary, LCL).

24. Nagle, *The Ancient World*, 51.

25. Pomeroy, *Women in Antiquity*, 150. However, this is not to say that all women in antiquity were denied power in a political sense. In *The Limits of Participation: Women and Civic Life in the Greek East in the Hellenistic and Roman Periods*, R. Bremen writes, "In the cities of the Greek East, during the late Hellenistic and Roman periods, female members of local ruling elites played a prominent and visible role in public life" (Amsterdam: J. C. Gieben 1996), 1.

26. Dionysius of Halicarnassus, *Rom. Ant.* II.25.6-7 (Cary, LCL), emphasis added.

27. Dionysius of Halicarnassus, *Rom. Ant.* II.26.1 (Cary, LCL).

28. Dionysius of Halicarnassus, *Rom. Ant.* II.25.2 (Cary, LCL). For a more detailed description of all that this law entailed, see *Rom. Ant.* II.25.1. For more information regarding marital subordination, see Gaius, *Institutes*, 1.108-18, 136-37a.

29. Dionysius of Halicarnassus, *Rom. Ant.* II.26.1 (Cary, LCL).

30. Dionysius of Halicarnassus, *Rom. Ant.* II.25.7. Spurius Carvilius is recorded as the first to divorce his wife and incurs the wrath of the people for this act (see Dionysius of Halicarnassus, *Rom. Ant.* II.25.7).

31. Pomeroy, *Women in Antiquity*, 150.

32. Thomas, *Roman Law*, 412.

33. Dionysius of Halicarnassus, *Rom. Ant.*, II.26.4.

34. Dionysius of Halicarnassus, *Rom. Ant.*, II.26.4-5. The sphere of authority of the *paterfamilias* over his son has been detailed here to shed light on the severity of his rule. One should not conclude that daughters have an easier time than sons, however. A conclusion of leniency toward daughters appears to be unfounded. Given the fact that a *paterfamilias* can kill his daughter if she is adulterous while under his power does not advocate any idea of leniency. Furthermore, given the nature of the time period, it is uncertain if the term "son" is limited to the masculine gender only. For example, Thomas writes of the *paterfamilias* being able to execute daughters as well as sons (*Roman Law*, 415) and B. Nicholas writes that the *paterfamilias* holds the "power of life or death" over his children in *An Introduction to Roman Law* (Clarendon Law Series; ed. H. L. A. Hart; Oxford: Oxford University Press, 1962), 65.

35. A. Borkowski, *Textbook on Roman Law* (Great Britain: Blackstone Press, 1994), 104.

36. Dionysius of Halicarnassus, *Rom. Ant.*, II.26.6 (Cary, LCL).

37. Dionysius of Halicarnassus, *Rom. Ant.*, II.27.1-2 (Cary, LCL), emphasis added. The successor of Romulus, Numa Pompilius, issues the following, thereby restricting the power of the father to sell his son: "If a father gives his son leave to marry a woman who by the laws is to be the sharer of his sacred rites and possessions, he shall no longer have the power of selling his son" (*Rom. Ant.* II.27.4; Cary, LCL).

38. Borkowski, *Roman Law*, 107.

39. Borkowski, *Roman Law*, 107.

40. Nicholas, *Introduction to Roman Law*, 80; cf. Borkowski, *Roman Law*, 107.

41. Augustus's hereditary rule continues until the death of Nero.

42. David Shotter, *Augustus Caesar* (Lancaster Pamphlets; eds. E. J. Evans and P. D. King; London: Routledge, 1991), 47.

43. Shotter, *Augustus*, 48. Augustus is esteemed after his death by succeeding emperors. The question can also be raised: "To what degree did future emperors 'keep the peace' by preserving the laws as given by Augustus, especially the attitude and laws concerning wives as echoed in *Roman Antiquities*?"

44. Shotter, *Augustus*, 46.

45. C. Freeman, *Egypt, Greece, and Rome: Civilizations of the Ancient Mediterranean* (New York: Oxford University Press, 1996), 382.

46. A. H. M. Jones, *Augustus*, (ed. M. I. Finley; New York: W. W. Norton & Company, 1970), 166. Note that this is the translation of the Latin: "*Romanos rerum dominos gentemque togatam*" as indicated by Jones, *Augustus*, 166.

47. Dio Cassius, *Roman History* 54.4-5 (E. Cary, LCL); cf. A. D. Winspear and L. K. Geweke, *Augustus and the Reconstruction of Roman Government and Society* (University of Wisconsin Studies in the Social Sciences and History 24; Madison: University of Wisconsin, 1935), 179-80.

48. Gell., *NA* 1.4.2 (J. C. Rolfe, LCL); cf. Suet., *Aug.* 89.2; Livy 59. According to A. C. Schlesinger, Aulus Gellius mistakenly credits the speech to Metellus Numidicus

rather than its true orator, Metellus Macedonicus (vol. 14 of Livy, page 66, footnote 1; LCL); cf. Winspear and Geweke, *Augustus and the Reconstruction*, 180.

49. Dionysius of Halicarnassus, *Rom. Ant.* II.25.4-5 (Cary, LCL).

50. Jones, *Augustus*, 166. While this quote in itself is not noteworthy, it does gain considerable merit by strengthening the basis of Augustus's positive disposition toward the past.

51. Jones, *Augustus*, 166.

52. Suet., *Aug.* 45.5 (Rolfe, LCL).

53. Jones, *Augustus*, 166.

54. Jones, *Augustus*, 166.

55. Jones, *Augustus*, 166.

56. Gell., *NA* 1.4.2 (Rolfe, LCL).

57. Winspear and Geweke, *Augustus and the Reconstruction*, 180.

58. Dio Cassius, *Roman History* 54.4-5 (Cary, LCL).

59. Cato as specified here is either Marcus Porcius Cato (234-149 BC) also known as "Cato the Elder" or Marcus Porcius Cato (95-46 BC) also known as "Cato the Younger."

60. Jones, *Augustus*, 166.

61. Macrob., *Sat.* (trans. P. V. Davies; New York: Columbia University Press, 1969), II.4.18.

62. Cato is Marcus Porcius Cato.

63. Young, *Anthology of Sacred Texts*, 167.

64. Young, *Anthology of Sacred Texts*, 167.

65. Young, *Anthology of Sacred Texts*, 167. Young does not specifically note or give any allusion to the danger that is meant here. It can only be logically deduced from the uproar that resulted on behalf of women.

66. Young, *Anthology of Sacred Texts*, 167.

67. Young, *Anthology of Sacred Texts*, 167.

68. Young, *Anthology of Sacred Texts*, 167.

69. Young, *Anthology of Sacred Texts*, 167.

70. Young, *Anthology of Sacred Texts*,167-68, emphasis added.

71. Livy 34.3 (Sage, LCL).

72. Dio Cassius, *Roman History* 56.10 (Scott-Kilvert).

73. Pomeroy, *Women in Antiquity*, 157 (referencing Ulp., *Dig.* 1.12); cf. M. R. Lefkowitz and M. B. Fant, *Women's Life in Greece and Rome: A Source Book in Translation* (2nd ed.; Baltimore: John Hopkins University Press, 1992), 111. Ulpian (*On Betrothal* 23.1.12.1), records that a daughter "is free to disagree [with her father] only if her father chooses for her a fiancé who is unworthy or of bad character" (Lefkowitz and Fant, *Women's Life*, 111).

74. Pomeroy, *Women in Antiquity*, 163.

75. Pomeroy, *Women in Antiquity*, 151.

76. Pomeroy, *Women in Antiquity*, 151.

77. Dio Cassius, *Roman History* 50.28 (Scott-Kilvert), emphasis added.

78. Balch, *Wives*, 71.

79. See *Roman History* 50.27.7.

80. Pomeroy, *Women in Antiquity*, 159.

81. Pomeroy, *Women in Antiquity*, 159, referencing *Dig.* 48.5.1-4.
82. Winspear and Geweke, *Roman Law*, 183, referencing *Dig.* 4.4.37.
83. Ulpian is in power from late second century and the beginning of the third century, technically from AD 193-213. He serves under five Roman emperors: Severus (193-211), Caracalla and Macrinus (211-18), and Elagabal and Alexander (218-23) as given by Tony Honoré, *Ulpian* (Oxford: Clarendon Press, 1982), 15, 25, and 33.
84. *Dig.* 48.5.14(13).5, as referenced by Pomeroy, *Women in Antiquity*, 159.
85. Pomeroy, *Women in Antiquity*, 160.
86. Pomeroy, *Women in Antiquity*, 160, referencing *Dig.* 48.5.6.1.
87. Suet., *Aug.* 101.4.
88. Kyme Aretalogy.
89. Jones, *Augustus*, 148; cf. Donaldson, *Cult of Isis*, 131.
90. Hooper, *Roman Realities*, 333.
91. Donalson, *Cult of Isis*, 131.
92. Donalson, *Cult of Isis*, 131.
93. Jones, *Augustus*, 148.
94. Jones, *Augustus*, 144.
95. Kee, *Early Christian World*, 129.
96. Kee, *Early Christian World*, 129.
97. Pomeroy, *Women in Antiquity*, 224.
98. Roullet, *Egyptianizing Monuments of Imperial Rome*, 2.
99. Roullet, *Egyptianizing Monuments of Imperial Rome*, 2.
100. Roullet, *Egyptianizing Monuments of Imperial Rome*, 38. Despite the dilemma that Roullet does not give a date for this occurrence, this fact is weighty since it does demonstrate the significance of Rome in terms of the Isiac religion.
101. Roullet, *Egyptianizing Monuments of Imperial Rome*, 2.
102. Pomeroy, *Women in Antiquity*, 225. However, according to Roullet, *Egyptianizing Monuments of Imperial Rome*, the temple had been destroyed under Tiberius and "probably rebuilt under Caligula" (23). Nevertheless, most sources credit Caligula for building the temple; thus, it is not in prior existence.
103. Roullet, *Egyptianizing Monuments of Imperial Rome*, 23.
104. Roullet, *Egyptianizing Monuments of Imperial Rome*, 2.
105. deTraci Regula, *The Mysteries of Isis: Her Worship and Magick*, (Llewellyn's World Religion and Magick Series; St Paul: Llewellyn Publications, 1995), 40.
106. Regula, *Mysteries of Isis*, 221
107. Regula, *Mysteries of Isis*, 221.
108. Roullet, *Egyptianizing Monuments of Imperial Rome*, 2. Nero is notorious for his harsh treatment of the Christians, persecuting them from AD 64 until his death on June 9th, 68 (W. Grudem, *The First Epistle of Peter: An Introduction and Commentary*, TNTC; Leicester: Inter-Varsity, 1988, 35). Nero is also one who might be classified as raised against the ideals of Christianity for he is "born of murderous parents, and brought up in a murderous atmosphere" (M. Grant, *Nero*; New York: Dorset Press, 1989, 13). However, Nero's upbringing certainly does not excuse the poisoning of his rival Britannicus or the murder of his mother Agrippina. Nor does it excuse using the Christians as a scapegoat for the great fire of Rome in AD 64, where

he coats them with wax and sets them on fire, to name one form of his persecutions against them. The Christians are known for being a strange group of people who are accused of incest, cannibalism, and refuse "to perform any religious obligation to the Roman gods," which excludes them from the army and the government (Hooper, *Roman Realities*, 387).

109. Roullet, *Egyptianizing Monuments of Imperial Rome*, 2.

110. Roullet, *Egyptianizing Monuments of Imperial Rome*, 2, referencing A. Hermann, *Jahrbuch für Antike und Christentum*, III (1960), 35-41.

111. Regula, *Mysteries of Isis*, 53.

112. Roullet, *Egyptianizing Monuments of Imperial Rome*, 2.

113. Roullet, *Egyptianizing Monuments of Imperial Rome*, 2 and 23.

114. Roullet, *Egyptianizing Monuments of Imperial Rome*, 2.

115. Roullet, *Egyptianizing Monuments of Imperial Rome*, 2.

Chapter Three

The Relevance of Isis to New Testament Studies

This chapter will demonstrate that the Isis cult provides a significant backdrop for the study of the New Testament, particularly the Pauline epistles. The archaeological evidence from the Isis cult preexists Christianity in many cases and is evident in the cities that Paul visits on his missionary journeys. This is not to say that the Isis cult is the only religion that Paul may have encountered or the only religion of this time period. In a syncretistic age, the Isis cult is one of the mystery religions which comes into popularity. People view Isis as a caring goddess who promises to give her devotees eternal life and help them with their woes in life. This can be seen in stark contrast to the Roman state religion which is designed to usher in peace and prosperity for the Roman state.

THE SPREAD OF THE ISIS RELIGION

Accessibility and Attraction of the Isis Cult

Unlike other cults that require special restrictions and screen initiates by "families, clans, or classes," mystery religions, including the Isis cult, are open to all.[1] Romans have the advantage of worshiping the gods that they chose due to the "inclusiveness of the polytheistic system."[2] When the state religion of Rome fails to cater to the needs of the people, mystery religions fill the void. The Isis cult also takes residence among those migrating into the Greco-Roman world. Jones writes that the immigrants of Rome, both "slave and free, who formed a large percentage of the population, naturally tended to cling to the gods of their various homelands."[3] Isis holds an attraction to the "indigenous Romans,"[4] and the influx of immigrants provides alternatives to the Roman inhabitants of the empire.[5]

While the religion of the Roman state is designed to bolster its peace and prosperity, the Isis cult addresses the personal needs of the populace. People

[margin note: Isis fulfills psychological needs]

have "psychological needs" which include "a feeling of helplessness before fate, uncertainty about the hereafter, curiosity about the supernatural and a sense of the instability of human affairs."[6] In contrast to the impersonal religion of the state, (which does not address these needs), the devotee of Isis experiences "the sacred" and is also guaranteed "personal security" by being incorporated into a religious system by "the corresponding personal closeness" of the goddess.[7]

The Isis Cult as a Backdrop for Paul's Missionary Journeys

Witt demonstrates in *Isis in the Ancient World* that the archaeological evidence (literary and numismatic) for the Isis cult corresponds with that of Paul's missionary journeys.[8] These cities (and provinces) include Ephesus, Tarsus, Mysia, Thessalonica, Athens, Corinth, Phrygia, Galatia, Macedonia, Philippi, Troas, and Rome.[9] However, archaeological evidence for the Isis cult is found throughout the Greco-Roman world with the majority of the evidence preceding a Christian date.[10] F. Dunand also charts archaeological evidence of the Isis cult in the "Diffusion du Culte Isiaque en Asie Mineure et en Syrie" which offers promising evidence of Isiac archaeological evidence in the forms of altars (or dedications), sanctuaries, coins, and figures of monuments along the Aegean Sea.[11] Because of the overlap of archaeological evidence of the Isis cult with the location of Paul's missionary journeys, it is appropriate to examine the beliefs of the Isis cult in correlation with those that Paul advocates.

ISIAC BELIEFS AND PRACTICES COMPARABLE TO PAUL

Isis: A Suffering and Benevolent Goddess

As manifest from the character of Isis in *Metamorphoses*, Isis comes to the aid of those who seek her help. Lucius identifies Isis's compassion as the care of a mother to the woes of those less fortunate in life.[12] Isis is also believed to exercise authority of the course of human life as it is thought to be "wholly governed by her providence."[13] The example of Isis freeing Lucius from his form as a donkey illustrates that Isis cares about the trials of people.

[margin note: suffering deity]

In other primary accounts of Isis, such as those by Diodorus and Plutarch, Isis experiences much loss. Isis loses her husband, searches for the torn parts of his body, and suffers when her husband has an affair with her sister, resulting in a child that Isis raises. Táckas comments, "Isis appealed to the depressed classes of the Roman empire, for the goddess knew what suffering meant."[14] This contrasts with other gods and goddesses who were more concerned with helping individuals after death.[15] By becoming an initiate into the Isis cult, one could enter into "a life of present security lived under the protection of a kindly mother goddess."[16] Perhaps the benevolence of Isis can be paralleled to the kindness of God in the New Testament, and the role of suffering that Isis endures to the suffering that Christ exhibits for his followers.

Isis as a Savior Goddess

As expressed in the account of Isiac initiation in *Metamorphoses*, Isis is believed to bestow eternal life upon her devotees. In *Metamorphoses*, the initiate Lucius recognizes Isis as the "holy and eternal saviour" of humankind.[17] "Both the gates of death and the guardianship of life were in the goddess's [Isis's] hands, and the act of initiation was performed in the manner of voluntary death and salvation by favour."[18] If those who have ended the days of their lives can be entrusted with the "great unspoken mysteries of the cult," then they are enabled to be "reborn through her providence and set once more upon the course of renewed life."[19]

H. Koester writes concerning mystery religions,

> Parallels with Christian statements abound in this narration [the initiation account in *Metamorphoses*] of an initiation into a mystery religion. One should not deny that the New Testament and the mysteries often speak the same language. When Paul says that those who have been baptized have died with Christ and should, therefore, walk in a new life, his words closely resemble those of the initiation into the Isis mysteries. That the Christians can also expect eternal life after they have been raised from the dead does not constitute a difference from the Isis mystery, because the devotees of Isis also know that they are not condemned to become unconscious shadows after death. The differences lie elsewhere: the initiation into the mysteries of Isis—and that is also true of other mystery religions—was reserved for only a few elect persons, i.e. to those who were able to pay the rather high expenses associated with initiation.[20]

Despite the similarities between the Isis cult and those of Christianity, noted by a New Testament scholar, a paucity of Isis discussion exists on the New Testament level. While some discussion of Isis exists on an archaeological level, archaeologists (such as Witt) are often at a loss to successfully incorporate their evidence with the New Testament. More work should be done to successfully solidify some of his arguments.[21]

Baptism in the Isis Cult

In the account of *Metamorphoses*, the devotee Lucius takes a customary bath upon his initiation into the Isis cult, witnessed by the devotees of Isis.[22] This is then followed with "purificatory sprinkling."[23] K. Barth considers this initiation rite to be a kind of baptism into the Isis cult.[24] Barth is not alone in his view. Tertullian also writes in his treatise on baptism of followers being "initiated into certain sacred rites by a bath,"[25] since the Romans "had for long been thoroughly familiar with the foreign cults," such as Isis.[26]

Archaeologist Witt testifies for the practice of baptism in the Isis cult, saying, "Certainly in the Isiac mysteries . . . a preliminary baptism was indispensable."[27] However, the practice of washing was known in other mystery religions as well. In "The Christian Mystery and the Pagan Mysteries," H. Rahner confirms the prevalence of washing in the mystery religions: "We know of an ablution in the ritual of Eleusis; the laurel-wreath oration of Demosthenes speaks of purificatory ablutions in the mystery of Sabazius; the cult of Attis had its taurobolium, and the *mystery of Isis knew a sanctifying baptismal bath*, so did the mysteries of Dionysus and Mithras."[28] So like other mystery religions, the initiation ceremony into the Isis cult can be considered a baptism comparable to that of Christianity.

In Egyptian history, this "rite of baptism" into the Isis cult is performed by the priest.[29] In the account of Lucius's initiation into the cult, the rite of baptism is described, illuminating the historicity of this account. Similarly, the last book of the *Ephesiaca*, detailing the life of a fisherman with the name Aegialeus, contains "unmistakable Isiac symbolism."[30] From this account, the allegorical meaning is drawn: "For the faithful follower of Isis the fish is taken out of the water just as the initiate is removed from the water in which he has been *ceremonially dipped*."[31]

Archaeological Evidence for Water Facilities in Iseums

R. Wild has studied the sanctuaries for the Isis cult firsthand and has written of his findings in *Water in the Cultic Worship of Isis and Sarapis*. Wild's work provides a comprehensive overview of the use of water in these cults and thus is an invaluable resource, while also being a primary source. This work, for my purposes, will only be utilized for the evidence of water facilities in the Iseums where Isis was worshiped. The status of the sanctuaries of Isis and their "permanent water facilities" have been preliminarily assessed in table 3.1 as follows:[32]

Table 3.1. Status of Permanent Water Facilities in Iseums for Cultic Purposes

	Water Facilities Present for Cultic Purposes	Water Facilities "Probably or Certainly Present"[33] for Cultic Purposes	Water Facilities "Possibly Present"[34] for Cultic Purposes
Hellenistic Period		Ephesus: State Agora (I-S?) Pompeii	Soli: Temple D
Roman Period	Aquileia (I-S?) Faesulae (I-S?) Lambaesis (I-S?)	Frauenberg (I-S?) Pergamum	Cyme Cyrene: Apollo Precinct Industria (I-S?) Ras el Soda Soli: Temple E

Wild discusses some of the questionable sites to attempt to arrive at a definitive answer in the use of water in these facilities. For example, in Ras el Soda (Egypt), a "water channel or drain" is present in the Iseum that might have served to "drain off waste water from a room used for ablution rites."[36] At Soli, the Iseum (known as Temple D) from the first century BC contains a water channel that runs between it and the temple of Aphrodite.[37] While one of these basins can be directly attributed to the worship of Aphrodite (since it remains within her sanctuary), the outer basin is believed to be for the use of those who visit the Iseum.[38]

The Cyme site had "une vaste citerne creusée dans le roc, recouverte d'un enduit épais, et un distributeur d'eau avec des tuyaux d'argile conduisait l'eau dans toutes les directions."[39] In other words, the sanctuary of Isis at Cyme has evidence for a cistern. Wild comments that this may be a

water *collection* system with its network of pipes serving to channel rainwater from either the roofs or the courtyard floor into a central tank. If the cistern mentioned was fed by a system of pipes and is located again in front of the main temple, it may have very well served certain cultic needs of this precinct.[40]

Industria may also have had an Isis-Sarapis sanctuary. Although Wild does not draw this conclusion, he notes that others have concluded that the well discovered may have offered water for initiation rites.[41]

An Isiac temple located "on the south side of the precinct of Apollo at Cyrene"[42] offers more promising evidence for it contains "an open tile drain."[43] The drain is located "on the floor in front of the cult platform of this Iseum," and offers "reasonable possibility" for holding a metal basin.[44]

In Eretria a dedication to Isis has been found dating to approximately 300 BC by some Egyptians."[45] According to N. G. Papadakis, this site is an Iseum; Wild concludes that "clearly this attribution is based on *SIRIS* 73,"[46] and later authors agree on this attribution.[47] The site in Eretria does contain a "water room," which is given a "waterproof tile floor" before 150 BC.[48]

However, after delving into the sites more, Wild arrives at a new interpretation of the evidence which involves reclassification. His data can be simplified as follows in table 3.2:[49]

Table 3.2.   Iseums with Water Facilities

	Sanctuaries of Isis with "cultic water facilities"[50]
Hellenistic Period	Ephesus: State Agora; Pompeii; Soli D
Roman Period	Cyme (I-S?); Cyrene: Apollo Precinct (I-S?); Frauenberg;[51] Pergamum

Overview of the Archaeological Evidence with Water Facilities

To best understand the use of water facilities in the Isis cult, table 3.3 has been utilized.

From table 3.3, it can be understood that water played a role in the Isis cult. This may have been used for ablution rituals, such as sprinkling. Or, water may have been utilized to create the "flood" effect of the Nile. The Nile is viewed as the sustenance of life, whose floods are critical for the fertility of the soil. The recreation of the flooding of the Nile is important to the Egyptians.

Interpreting the Archaeological Evidence

In attempting to decipher through the technicalities of Wild's research, a few generalizations can be drawn. First, it is evident that water facilities are present in Iseums. The question as detailed in table 3.3 is not whether such facilities are present; it is simply how the facilities are used. If these water facilities are used in the rituals of the Isis cult, then evidence may be gathered for baptism. Wild has done research involving crypts utilized in the sanctuaries, such as that used in Pompeii for the Isis cult. Concerning the facility in Pompeii, some argue that the crypt is designed for the purpose of bathing or for "ritual ablutions."[57] Whatever the function and use for this crypt, baptism for the Isis cult remains a possible explanation of the archaeological evidence.

Striking is the flood effect purposefully produced with water overflowing the water basins. This may be comparable to descriptions of Christian baptism facilities. According to *Didache* 7, "living water" (or the water found in moving bodies, such as rivers, seas, or springs), is to be utilized in baptism.[58] Also, the Latin word *fons*, or a "spring or source of flowing water," is the name for the "baptismal basin."[59] Baptismal basins often try to imitate the living water idea by arranging a "system of pipes through which the baptismal water flowed into the basin."[60]

However, the support of archaeological evidence is not critical to sustaining the validity of the initiation account of Lucius. The customary bath that Lucius takes is not said to have been taken in the temple itself nor is the act of sprinkling performed within the temple. When Lucius first approaches Isis, he dunks his head seven times in the sea before praying to the goddess.[61] As Wild states, ablution rites "clearly did not require a fixed facility within the sanctuary."[62] Neither of these accounts necessitate the archaeological evidence of baptismal fonts within temples to substantiate their claims.

In other words, just because an Iseum does not have a water basin does not indicate that ablution rites are not practiced in the Isis cult. Wild states, "Clearly the absence of a basin at a given site does not mean that ablution rites were not practiced there."[63] Thus, although archaeological support for water initiation rites is helpful, it need not be present indisputably at every site.

The question can be raised: Does baptism exist in the Isis cult? When analyzing the above evidence, I would say the answer is absolutely. The witness of Tertullian, coupled with the initiation of Lucius, and bolstered by archaeological evidence which attest to the use of water in Isiac temples helps to foster this conclusion.

ISIS AND OSIRIS AND RESURRECTION

Another parallel between the Isis cult and the New Testament is resurrection. This idea is alluded to by Plutarch. In his account, Isis weeps over her beloved husband who has died.[64] In referring only to the lamentation of Isis, Plutarch might be referencing the *entire* lamentation process,[65] including the spells of Isis used to raise Osiris from the dead.[66] In this manner, the lamentation exhibited would be one step in a series of rituals, the final ritual (being the exclamations spoken over Osiris's body) imparts new life. In the *Pyramid Texts* and *The Lamentations of Isis and Nepthys*, both Isis and her sister lament Osiris. However, "in the course of time the bitter dirges came to be the sole province of Isis,"[67] which is recorded in Plutarch's account. C. J. Bleeker comments on the lamentation as containing "the force of the magical world" and being "a spell which raises Osiris from death."[68] Budge highlights the importance of Isis's role in the resurrection of Osiris,

> If we consider the part played by Isis in the history of Osiris, we shall find that without her help Osiris must have perished. It was Isis who searched out and collected the members of his mutilated body, and presided over its constitution. It was Isis who uttered the spells which revivified his body . . . and made him to have union with her after his death and beget their son Horus.[69]

In a sense, then, Osiris can not be the famous god that he is without the help of his wife. Without Isis, also, Osiris's son Horus would not have been born. In some versions of the Isis myth, she causes the body of Osiris to be revived to impregnate her.[70]

Osiris as a Fertility (Vegetation) God and Resurrection God[71]

In order to understand Isis thoroughly, it is critical to understand her husband Osiris. The belief in Osiris as "the resurrected one" finds its way into Egyptian society because of his function as the god of vegetation. Plutarch labels Osiris as a fertility god for Osiris was "the whole source and faculty creative of moisture, believing this to be the cause of generation and the substance of life-producing seed."[72]

Table 3.3. Overview of Archaeological Evidence for Water Facilities in Iseums[52]

Isiac Site	Date Founded	Water Facilities	Dimensions	Possible Function	Miscellaneous
Cenchreae	2nd century AD?	Fountain			Some believe this is the sanctuary of the Iseum described in Metamorphoses.
Cyrene: Apollo District	117-38 AD (?)	Drain in center of cult platform (ca. 200 AD)		Basin for ablution rituals	
*Ephesus: State Agora	50-1 BC	Square water basin which may have served as a washing facility (ca. 200 AD)	1.2 m by 1.8 m Depth = .18 m	Sprinkling basin	Drain and inflow pipe included
Eretria	Ca. 300 BC	Water room with a well	3.3 m square	Nile water facility; ablution rituals	Waterproof tile is added before 150 BC; well taps into Nile water
*Frauenberg	Late 1st century–early second century AD	Large water basin (outside temple)	Exterior: ca. 2.9 m by 2.6 m Interior: ca. 1.9 m by 1.5 m	Receiving basin for water; re-enactment of the Nile flood	Basin contains opening for reaching water; fed by a water channel, carrying rain water from temple roof
Pergamum	Early 2nd century AD	Cistern Low, flat basin	Depth = 4 m 11.3 m by 5.2 m Depth = .22m	Water source Sprinkling basin	Located underground No drain/inflow pipe
		Deep basin	11.3 m by 1.4 m	Water basin, recreates the Nile flood	Inflow for water line
		Ornamental basins			Located in courtyards

Philae	None given	Four Nilometers		Located along Nile
Pompeii	2nd century BC	Crypt in courtyard (underground)	ca.3.2 m by 2.8 m (exterior) 2.5 m by 2.2 m (interior) 2 m by 1.5 m (int. room)	Water would flow into the basin and onto the floor recreating the "flood" effect. This site resembles a Nilometer.
		Platform for a water jar Water basin	.85 m by 1.5 m	The water basin and water jar are contained in the underground crypt. (A sacristy and meeting room or ecclesiasterion are also present.)
Rome: Santa Sabina	Late 2nd century AD	Bathing facility established in 3rd century (transformed from a meeting room).		

Osiris has been described by some as the "classical example of the dying and rising god of vegetation."[73] He is especially identified with the corn harvest. He becomes associated with the god Neper (a grain god in Egypt) and eventually the attributes of Neper are "absorbed by Osiris."[74] As the grain or corn god, Osiris also became associated with the resurrection of those who had died. Furthermore, "The germination of the grain typified the germination of the spirit-body of the deceased."[75]

The corn-mummy helps to demonstrate the connection Egyptians make between Osiris and vegetation. According to J. Griffiths, "In the late era an effigy of the god [Osiris] was sometimes made of earth and in it seeds were placed which eventually sprouted, thus indicating the renewed life of the god."[76] Another custom which is implemented in the New Kingdom is the use of the "Osiris-bed" where the burial chamber contained a wooden frame with a papyrus mat atop of which was a cloth "on which a bed of mould was laid, modeled in the shape of the Osiris effigy."[77] Instead of corn being planted, barley is sown with the same idea being represented.[78]

Foundational for these conclusions is the evidence for a figure of Osiris buried in the tomb of Tutankhamûn. This custom, also found in later tombs, consists of "a wooden frame moulded in the form of that god [Osiris], hallowed out, lined with linen, filled with silt from the Nile bed, and planted with corn."[79] "Bandaged in the like manner as a mummy," this has become known as an "Osiris bed."[80] Brandon suggests that the seeds of corn were intended "to assist, by means of imitative magic, in achieving the resurrection of the dead person, buried in the tomb, to a new life."[81]

Evidence for the association of Osiris with the resurrection of the dead continues on in the Egyptian populace in the form of mortuary rituals. Budge observes, "No funerary inscription exists, however early, in which evidence cannot be found proving that the deceased had set his hope of immortality in Osiris, and at no time in Egypt's long history do we find that the position of Osiris was usurped by any other god."[82] Indeed, Osiris is recognized by Egyptians as "the great type and symbol of the Resurrection."[83] Originally, merely revered as a man who has attained resurrection from the dead, for the Egyptian populace Osiris becomes much more. Osiris becomes the "*cause* of the resurrection of the dead" for "the power to bestow eternal life upon mortals was transferred from the gods to him."[84]

Burial rituals relating to Osiris involve people placing Osiris figures made from damp soil mixed with seed in tombs of the deceased.[85] The seed will sprout within the tomb, serving as a symbol for "new life rising from the dead Osiris."[86] This custom continues into the time of Christianity.[87]

The belief of the resurrection of Osiris is also celebrated in festivals. One of these is the "annual Festival of Khoiakh, which celebrated Osiris's death and resurrection" and is "performed in major towns throughout Egypt."[88] This festival links the rise to power of the current ruler with Osiris's resurrection. It also celebrates the flood of the Nile and "renewal of the vegetation."[89]

Another festival, held at Abydos honors the major events in Osiris's "life, death, and resurrection."[90] The focus of this festival is a ritual called the "Raising of the *Djed*-pillar," in which this pillar is raised from the ground or a horizontal position to a vertical position.[91] In some of these ceremonies, the pillar is made to resemble Osiris by adorning it with clothes, a crown, arms (to hold a scepter), and drawn eyes.[92]

The Egyptians hold to the belief that "their bodies would vanquish the powers of death, and the grave, and decay, because Osiris had vanquished them."[93] Men long to be buried near the presence of Osiris (who is believed to buried in Abydos) so mummies of the wealthy are transported to this location.[94] Thus, because the myth of Osiris involves Osiris rising "in a transformed spiritual body," people have confidence "of the resurrection in an immortal, eternal, and spiritual body."[95]

Isis's Role in Resurrection

Isis's part in Egyptian resurrection beliefs is also important. In the harvest festivals, Isis is the one who is credited with having the power to resurrect the grain, and praise is given to her.[96] Isis also plays an important role in funerary rituals for the deceased. Her lamentations over Osiris's death are incorporated into funeral rites. R. David notes, "Lamentations were a part of the funerary rites intended to save the dead from the absolute death or 'second death' that was reserved for the wicked or those who had not made the necessary funeral preparations."[97] The Egyptian populace believe weeping like Isis would set in motion the resurrection of their loved one as Isis's weeping does for Osiris.[98] Because of this belief, a "special form of lamentation" is used in the cult of the dead which include rites that are part of the Osiris cult.[99] In the cult of Osiris, two wailing women (Isis and Nephthys) weep over the death of Osiris. Hence, in processions to the funeral for deceased Egyptians from "time immemorial," two individuals identified as Isis and her sister take part in the procession as weeping women.[100] Bleeker describes them as follows:

> That these two wailing-women actually represented the divine sisters appears from the opening passage of 'The Songs of Isis and Nephthys,' which reads: 'Two women should be fetched, pure of body, virgins, the hair of whose bodies has been shaved off, round whose heads braids have been plaited, whose hands hold a tambourine and on whose upper arms their names have been written, viz. Isis and Nephthys.[101]

Isis's seeking and finding of Osiris is also incorporated into an Egyptian resurrection ritual called the *"Discovery of Osiris,"*[102] a six-day public performance enacting her search for the body of Osiris held annually beginning October 28 and ending on November 3.[103] According to Firmicus Maternus's narration of the event, the parts of dismembered Osiris, who is recognized as an "idol," are buried and lamented over.[104] On the final night, the public rejoices over the finding (revival) of Osiris's body, shouting refrains of victory such as "Osiris has been found" or "We have found, and rejoice."[105] Those in the countryside also participate in the festivities, singing and dancing "for the rediscovered Osiris gives life to the seeds of future harvests."[106]

Scholars differ about whether it is the weeping of Isis or the "finding" of Osiris that should be linked to resurrection in these festival rituals. The "finding" of Osiris's body parts and raising them from the ground on the last day of the festival seems more likely.

CONCLUSION

This chapter has accomplished a number of goals. First, the Isis cult has been shown to be present in many of the cities located on Paul's missionary journeys. Second, similar concepts to those in the New Testament have been identified. These include salvation, suffering, baptism, and resurrection. Osiris as the "resurrected one" has been detailed here to provide a complete picture along with Isis as a notable element in popular Egyptian resurrection beliefs and rituals. In the next chapter, the issues of salvation, baptism, resurrection, and freedom in Pauline Christianity will be compared with those of Isis.

NOTES

1. S. A. Takács, *Isis and Sarapis in the Roman World* (Religions in the Graeco-Roman World 124; eds. R. Van Den Broek et al.; Leiden: E. J. Brill, 1995), 8.

2. Takács, *Isis and Sarapis*, 16.

3. Jones, *Augustus*, 144.

4. Jones, *Augustus*, 144.

5. Takács, *Isis and Sarapis*, 17.

6. E. Ferguson, "Religions, Greco-Roman," *DLNT*, 1007.

7. W. Burkert, *Ancient Mystery Cults*, Carl Newell Jackson Lectures (Cambridge: Harvard University Press, 1987), 11.

8. See Witt, *Isis in the Ancient World*, 264-65.

9. Evidence for Rome is found in Witt, *Isis in the Ancient World*, 56-57. The list as presented here is not intended to be exhaustive.

10. See Witt, *Isis in the Ancient World*, 265-66; cf. 56-57.

11. See F. Dunand (*Le culte d'Isis le bassin oriental de la Méditerranée*; EPRO 26; Leiden: E. J. Brill, 1973, 3: carte 1). This evidence is of importance particularly

when tracking Paul's third missionary journey and to a somewhat lesser extent, his second missionary journey.

12. Apul., *Metam.* 11.25.

13. Apul., *Metam.* 11.3 (Hanson, LCL).

14. Takács, *Isis and Sarapis*, 4.

15. LiDonnici, "Women's Religions," 89-90.

16. Willoughby, *Pagan Regeneration*, 193.

17. Apul., *Metam.* 11.25 (Hanson, LCL).

18. Apul., *Metam.* 11.21 (Hanson, LCL).

19. Apul., *Metam.* 11.21 (Hanson, LCL).

20. H. Koester, *History, Culture, and Religion of the Hellenistic* Age (vol. 1 of *Introduction to the New Testament;* Philadelphia; Fortress Press, 1984), 191.

21. Roullet also does extensive work regarding the Isis cult in *The Egyptian and Egyptianizing Monuments of Imperial Rome*, but fails to intertwine her evidence with the biblical text.

22. Apul., *Metam.* 11.23.

23. Apul., *Metam.* 11.23 (Hanson, LCL).

24. K. Barth, *The Epistle to the Romans* (trans. from the sixth edition by E. C. Hoskyns; London: Oxford University Press, 1965), 192. According to Barth, the cults of Mithras and Cybele also practice baptism as an initiation rite.

25. Tert., *Tertullian's Treatises: Concerning Prayer, Concerning Baptism* (Latin Text; Series II of Translations of Christian Literature; trans. A. Souter; London: Society of Promoting Christian Knowledge, 1919), ch. 5.

26. Tert., *Tertullian's Treatises*, ch. 5, footnote 1.

27. Witt, *Isis in the Ancient World*, 160.

28. H. Rahner, "The Christian Mystery and the Pagan Mysteries" in *The Mysteries: Papers from the Eranos Yearbooks* (Bollingen Series 30, vol. 2 of *Papers from the Eranos Yearbooks*; ed. J. Campbell; trans R. Manheim; Princeton: Princeton University Press, 1955), 388, emphasis added.

29. Witt, *Isis in the Ancient World*, 22, referencing Tert., *De Baptismo* 5: *FRA* 381, 21-22.

30. *RMA*, 108, as cited by Witt, *Isis in the Ancient World*, 250.

31. Witt, *Isis in the Ancient World*, 250, emphasis added.

32. This chart has been adapted from Wild, *Water in the Cultic Worship*, 9.

33. Wild, *Water in the Cultic Worship*, 10.

34. Wild, *Water in the Cultic Worship*, 10.

35. (I-S?) designates the possibility of an Isis-Sarapis sanctuary. However, this should not be deemed problematic because Sarapis pales in comparison to that of Isis. Sarapis is simply an "entourage" of Isis and "yield[s] first place to her" (Koester, *Introduction to the New Testament*, 188).

36. Wild, *Water in the Cultic Worship*, 11-12. However, Wild notes that the water channel or drain may have had a secular function (*Water in the Cultic Worship*, 12). Nonetheless, while it may be difficult to pinpoint the exact function of such archaeological evidence, one should not overlook the evidence itself.

37. The date from Temple D has been gathered from the work of Strabo, 14.6.3, as given by Wild, *Water in the Cultic Worship*, 14.

38. Wild, *Water in the Cultic Worship*, 15.

39. Wild, *Water in the Cultic Worship*, 17, citing *BCH* 49 (1925), 478. My translation of this statement is as follows: "a vast cistern dug in the rock, covered with a thick coating, and a water distributor with clay pipes led water in all directions."

40. Wild, *Water in the Cultic Worship*, 17.

41. Wild, *Water in the Cultic Worship*, 17, citing Barra Bagnasco *et al.*, *Scavi*, 13, 26-27, 34-37.

42. Wild, *Water in the Cultic Worship*, 21

43. Wild, *Water in the Cultic Worship*, 21

44. Wild, *Water in the Cultic Worship*, 21. The metal basin may support evidence for ablution rites, such as baptism.

45. Wild, *Water in the Cultic Worship*, 175.

46. Wild, *Water in the Cultic Worship*, 175. *SIRIS* 73 is valuable evidence for the existence of the Isis cult at Eretria. According to Wild, *SIRIS* 73 is "the earliest of all the inscriptions" and consists of "a dedication to Isis" (*Water in the Cultic Worship*, 175).

47. Wild notes that these include Salditt-Trappmann, *Tempel*, 67; Auberon-Schefold, *Füher*, 139; Bruneau, *Sanctuaire*, 99-100, 116 (Wild, *Water in the Cultic Worship*, 266, footnote 80).

48. Wild, *Water in the Cultic Worship*, 116

49. This chart has been adapted from Wild, *Water in the Cultic Worship*, 23.

50. Wild, *Water in the Cultic Worship*, 23.

51. This site appears to more accurately classified as "questionable" based upon the analysis provided by Wild (*Water in the Cultic Worship*, 175-76).

52. This chart has been based upon Wild, *Water in the Cultic Worship*, 163-66, supplemented with corresponding information throughout the book. Questionable sites have been designated by an *.

53. Alternate dates that exist in this column, such as Cyrene and Ephesus, represent the fact that these cites are remodeled at a later date. Cyrene is remodeled in AD 211-27 and Ephesus in ca. AD 200 (Wild, *Water in the Cultic Worship*, 163-64, 171, 174).

54. Papadakis and subsequent scholars (Salditt-Trappmann, Auberon-Schefold, and Bruneau) attribute this site to Isis (Wild, *Water in the Cultic Worship*, 266, footnote 80).

55. A Nilometer measures the water of the Nile and also provides water (especially for the purposes of the cult). Nilometers consist of underground crypts with stairways and are established at the low water level of the Nile. Water flows from the soil or through a channel down into the crypt. The water depth of the river is measured by markings on the wall or by the steps themselves.

56. However, the *Ecclesiasterion* and the "Sacristy" do not come into being until after AD 62 (Wild, *Water in the Cultic Worship*, 180).

57. Wild, *Water in the Cultic Worship*, 51.

58. *Didache* 7 as cited in Wild, *Water in the Cultic Worship*, 50.

59. Wild, *Water in the Cultic Worship*, 50.

60. Wild, *Water in the Cultic Worship*, 50, citing Klausner, *Pisciculi*, 161-62.

61. Apul., *Metam.* 11.1.

62. Wild, *Water in the Cultic Worship*, 147.

63. Wild, *Water in the Cultic Worship*, 148.

64. Plut., *De Is. et Os.* 5.357 d.

65. That is, perhaps Plutarch is utilizing a synecdoche (simply speaking of the lamentation) to refer to the whole of the lamentation process (including the raising of Osiris).

66. Others assume the use of spells or magic by Isis in their narration of this myth. See Budge, *Egyptian Resurrection*, 2.279; R. David, *Religion and Magic in Ancient Egypt* (London: Penguin Books, 2002), 156.

67. Witt, *Isis in the Ancient World*, 41.

68. Bleeker, "The Saviour Goddess," 8.

69. Budge, *Osiris* 2:279.

70. G. Pinch, *Magic in Ancient Egypt* (Austin: University of Texas Press, 1994), 154.

71. Note that the concepts and ideas expressed in this section also relate to Osiris as a resurrection god since fertility, vegetation, and resurrection are intertwined in nature.

72. Plut., *De Is. et Os.* 364 a (Babbitt, LCL). Plutarch comments later that when Osiris is locked up in his coffin that this is nothing more than the "vanishing and disappearance of water" (*De Is. et Os.* 5.366 d; Babbit, LCL).

73. S. G. F. Brandon, "Vegetation Spirits," *MMM* 11:2939.

74. Budge, *Osiris*, 1:58.

75. Budge, *Osiris*, 1:58.

76. J. G. Griffiths, *The Origins of Osiris* (Münchner ägyptologische Studien 9; Berlin: Verlag Bruno Hessling, 1966), 109.

77. Griffiths, *The Origins of Osiris*, 109. However, only seven Osiris beds have actually been found (Shaw and Nicholson, "Osiris bed," *DAE*, 215).

78. Griffiths, *The Origins of Osiris*, 109, referring to Gardiner in Davies and Gardiner, *The Tomb of Amenemhet* (London, 1915), 115.

79. H. Carter, Vol. 3 of *The Tomb of Tut-ankh-amen: Discovered by the Late Earl of Carnarvon and Howard Carter* (New York: Cooper Square Publishers, 1963), citing Plate LXIV, A, 61.

80. Carter, Vol. 3 of *The Tomb of Tut-ankh-amen*, 61. Carter writes of the significance of this, saying, "It is but another example how, in that ancient funerary cult, the virtuous dead were identified in every possible way with Osiris" (Vol. 3 of *The Tomb of Tut-ankh-amen*, 61).

81. Brandon, "Vegetation Spirits," 11:2940.

82. Budge, *Osiris*, 1:1.

83. Budge, *Osiris*, 1:1.

84. Budge, *Egyptian Religion*, 83.

85. S. G. F. Brandon, "Osiris," *MMM* 8:2088.

86. Brandon, "Osiris," *MMM* 8:2088.

87. Firmicus Maternus finds this custom to be problematic since it existed simultaneously with Christianity (Donalson, *Cult of Isis*, 81). The popularity of this custom is also attested to by Rutilius Namatianus in *On His Return* or *De Suo Reditu* which

"recognized that the festival on November 3 was still very much alive" (Donalson, *Cult of Isis*, 81).

88. David, *Religion and Magic*, 157. This festival also celebrates Osiris as being named "king of the dead" (157).

89. David, *Religion and Magic*, 157.

90. David, *Religion and Magic*, 157.

91. David, *Religion and Magic*, 157.

92. David, *Religion and Magic*, 157. Nagel also writes of the *Djed* pillar being represented on a Theban tomb during the reign of Amenhotep III (1405-1370 BC) from the tomb of Kheriuf where the king raises the Djed pillar in the presence of the queen and princesses (" 'Mysteries' of Osiris," 126) which may further the belief of resurrection for Egyptian society since it is being promoted by the king in this account.

93. Budge, *Egyptian Religion*, 103.

94. Budge, *Egyptian Religion*, 103.

95. Budge, *Egyptian Religion*, 104.

96. Strouhal, *Ancient Egyptians*, 96.

97. David, *Religion and Magic*, 146.

98. Bleeker, "Saviour Goddess," 7.

99. Bleeker, "Saviour Goddess," 7.

100. Bleeker, "Saviour Goddess," 7, citing *Pyr.* 2092 a - 2093 b. Young also confirms that women imitated Isis and Nephthys in funerary rituals, but dates this to the Middle Kingdom period (*Anthology of Sacred Texts*, 127).

101. Bleeker, "Saviour Goddess," 7. Later on the role of lamenting is seen strictly as belonging to Isis (Witt, *Isis in the Ancient World*, 41).

102. Turcan, *Cults of the Roman Empire*, 118.

103. This account has been taken from Witt, *Isis in the Ancient World*, 162, 180.

104. Firm. Mat., *The Error of the Pagan Religions* (Ancient Christian Writers: The Works of the Fathers in Translation 37; ed. J. Quasten, W. J. Burghardt, T. Comerford Lawler, trans. C. A. Forbes, New York: Newman Press, 1970), 22.3. His words of the folly of this event are striking and deserve stating, "You bury an idol, you lament an idol, you bring forth from its sepulture an idol, and having done this, unfortunate wretch, you rejoice. You rescue your god, you put together the stony limbs that lie there, you set in position an insensible stone. Your god should thank you, should repay you with equivalent gifts, should be willing to make you his partner" (Firm. Mat., *Pagan Religions*, 22.3).

105. Witt, *Isis in the Ancient World*, 162.

106. Turcan, *Cults of the Roman Empire*, 118.

Chapter Four

Concepts in
Pauline Christianity Overlapping
with Concepts in the Isis Cult

This chapter will demonstrate that concepts existent in the Isis cult, such as freedom, salvation, resurrection, and baptism overlap with these same concepts in Pauline Christianity. With such similarities, the Isis cult and Pauline Christianity could draw some of the same people who are predisposed to these concepts. This chapter will develop this line of thought through examining works of biblical scholars on these particular concepts as well as comparing and contrasting them with those in the Isis cult.

PAULINE COMPARISONS WITH THE ISIS CULT

ἐλευθερία (f. nom. adj.)
ἐλεύθερος (m. nom.)
ἐλευθερόω

Freedom

Paul is an advocate of freedom in his ministry. Dunn states the necessity of "Christian liberty" for Paul to be of "fundamental importance."[1] This can be seen by examining Paul's vocabulary. J. K. Chamblin concludes that Paul's use of terms denoting liberation (ἐλευθερία, ἐλεύθερος, and ἐλευθερόω) with regard to the gospel is "confined to Galatians, 1-2 Corinthians and Romans; *but the concept of liberty permeates all the letters.*"[2] Paul uses these words *talks more* with more frequency than any other New Testament author, as table 4.1 details. It confirms that liberation is more central to Paul's thinking than for other New Testament authors. According to Dunn, " 'Liberation' and 'freedom' were important words and, more to the point, were important experiences for Paul and his converts."[3]

Paul's perspective on freedom is in part based on his unique conversion experience. J. M. Everts comments that Paul's "life and values were radically changed by his Damascus Road experience."[4] Paul could have been struck

71

Table 4.1. Paul's Usage of Words Denoting Freedom in Comparison with Other New Testament Authors

	Paul	Matthew	John	Peter	James	Total	Conclusion
ἐλευθερόω *to free*	Rom 6.18 Rom 6.22 Rom 8.2 Rom 8.21 Gal 5.1		John 8.32 John 8.36			Paul: 5 Others: 2	Paul utilizes ἐλευθερόω three more instances than other NT authors, or about 71% of all occurrences in the NT.
ἐλεύθερος (*n. m. s. adj.*) *free,* *unrestrained,* *unfettered*	Rom 6.20 Rom 7.3 1 Cor 7.21 1 Cor 7.22 1 Cor 7.39 1 Cor 9.1 1 Cor 9.19 1 Cor 12.1 Gal 3.28 Gal 4.22 Gal 4.23 Gal 4.26 Gal 4.30 Gal 4.31 Eph 6.8 Col 3.11	Mt 17.26	John 8.33 John 8.36 Rev 6.15 Rev 13.16 Rev 19.18	1 Pet 2.16	Paul: 16 Others: 7		Paul utilizes ἐλεύθερος nine more instances or about 70% of all occurrences in the NT.
ἐλευθερία *ας, ἡ* (*noun*) *liberty, freedom*	Rom 8.21 1 Cor 10.29 2 Cor 3.17 Gal 2.4 Gal 5.1 Gal 5.13a Gal 5.13b			1 Pet 2.16 2 Pet 2.19	Jas 1.25 Jas 2.12	Paul: 7 Others: 4	Paul utilizes ἐλευθερία three more instances or about 64% of all occurrences in the NT.

down for opposing God by his persecution of the church. Instead, he experiences God's bountiful grace and given a second chance at life.

Grace becomes a key component of Paul's message. Dunn determines that, along with love, grace is "at the centre of Paul's gospel."[5] God's grace on the Damascus Road frees Paul from dependence upon the law.

> Paul was converted to the position he had persecuted; he abandoned the law like those he had persecuted. If Paul's rationale is sought it can be readily guessed at: the law had approved the punishment of Jesus by death; but the Damascus road encounter revealed to Paul that God had vindicated this Jesus; therefore the law is a fool and should now be discarded. 'Christ is the end of the law!'[6]

As a Pharisee, Paul's loyalty to Jewish law is unquestionable. In the light of his personal experience of God's grace, he comes to see the law as a type of bondage that he now owes to Jesus Christ. Galatians 2.4 seems to draw out this antithesis, "But it was because of the false brethren secretly brought in, who had sneaked in to spy out our liberty [ἐλευθερίαν] which we have in Christ Jesus, in order to bring us into bondage [καταδουλώσουσιν]."[7] Καταδουλόω could literally be translated as "according to slavery."[8]

Paul fiercely guards his gospel of freedom from being reduced to bondage, which might be defined as anything besides the cross. In Gal 3.1, he chastises both the Judaizing false teachers and the Galatians on this point: "You foolish Galatians, who has bewitched you, before whose eyes Jesus Christ was publicly portrayed as crucified?" In Gal 1.8, he rebukes similarly: "But even if we, or an angel from heaven, should preach to you a gospel contrary to what we have preached to you, he is to be accursed!" Dunn comments, "He [Paul] converted from a zealous practitioner of the law to someone who warned his Gentile converts vehemently against the law (Gal 5.1-12)."[9]

Before his conversion, Paul views keeping the law as the best way to be justified before God. What he has regarded as a proper way of life (living by the law), loses its priority when he meets Christ. As Dunn notes, "The practice of the law, which had previously been his delight, he now regarded as a kind of slavery, the slavery of the spiritually immature."[10] Now he sees the law at its best as a παιδαγωγὸς to lead people to Christ. R. Longenecker explains, "It was the person and work of Jesus Christ as the fulfillment of Israel's hopes, and not an early dissatisfaction with the law, that made all the difference; thereby transforming the zealous Rabbi Saul into the zealous Apostle Paul."[11]

Galatians 2.16 is important for understanding this radical reversal:

> Nevertheless knowing that a man is not justified by the works of the law but through faith in Christ Jesus, even we have believed in Christ Jesus, so that we may be justified by faith in Christ and not by the works of the law; since by the works of the law no flesh will be justified.

This contrasts with his former approach, as he relates it in Gal 1.13-14, "For you have heard of my former manner of life in Judaism beyond many of my contemporaries among my countrymen, being more extremely zealous for my ancestral traditions." But what Paul once holds onto—the law—he grows to regard as a "yoke of slavery" (Gal 5.1), or "a yoke which neither our fathers nor we have been able to bear" (Acts 15.10). He admonishes those who seek to be justified by this yoke of slavery as having "fallen from grace" (Gal 5.4). Paul contrasts this yoke with grace as evident in Acts 15.11 by the word ἀλλά.[12] Acts 15.11 should literally read, "*But* we believe that we are saved through the grace of the Lord Jesus, in the same way as they also are."[13]

Not only is Paul liberated from the law, but he is also freed from the distinctions that circumscribe the law. That is, according to the law, people are differentiated as Jew and Greek (or Gentile). While Paul once holds to this distinction prior to his conversion experience, he no longer fosters this division in his epistles. For example, Paul says in Rom 10.12, "for there is no distinction between Jew and Greek;" in Gal 3.28, "there is neither Jew nor Greek;" and in Col 3.11,"There is no distinction between Greek and Jew, circumcised and uncircumcised." Rather, Christ is stressed as the unifying element among racial, ethnic, and cultural distinctions in these verses.

Paul's view of freedom entails not only ethnic freedom but also gender freedom. Equality is not limited to freedom from the law, but includes equality between both men and women. Galatians 3.28 reads, "There is neither Jew nor Greek, there is neither slave nor free man, there is neither male nor female; for you are all one in Christ Jesus." While some may regard this as strictly relating to one's "spiritual standing"[14] or trace it back to a "relation to baptism,"[15] Paul's view may have sociological implications for him as well.

Paul reference to Phoebe (Rom 16.1) is a crucial piece of evidence for Paul's acting on his convictions about gender freedom. Here, he commends Phoebe as a διάκονος, a word he also uses to describe his own ministry (1 Cor 3.5, 2 Cor 3.6, 2 Cor. 6.4, 2 Cor 11.23, Eph 3.7, Phil 1.1, Col 1.23, Col 1.25).[16] Classifying Phoebe as a deacon "points to her high status among the community" and seeing διάκονος in this light also fits with the letter of recommendation that Paul gives her.[17] Phoebe is given a "recommendation to the church in Rome that equals the recommendation given to Timothy as Paul's representative to Corinth."[18]

However since διάκονος is often translated as "servant,"[19] the true meaning of the word might be masked. Perhaps Phoebe is a deacon only in the specific sense of being an "intermediary or courier" or "one who serves as an intermediary in a transaction."[20] D. Moo mentions Phoebe as a letter carrier[21] of the book of Romans as a likely choice.[22] But "it is highly likely προστάτις also leader, protector, champion

— though not explicitly stated — that Phoebe was the letter carrier and authoritative interpreter for the Roman Christians as Paul's personal envoy." [23] *letter carrier — Paul's envoy* If Phoebe is seen as the letter carrier of the book of Romans, a view held by conservative Bible scholar J. MacArthur, this speaks volumes of Paul's view of women. [24]

In Dodd's estimation, Phoebe as Paul's letter carrier is "no insignificant claim" since Romans is "possibly the most important book" of the New Testament. [25] Besides the likelihood of being the letter carrier of the book of Romans, Phoebe is also identified as a προστάτις. A *hapax legomena*, προστάτις may refer to "patron" or "benefactor." If Paul is trying to denote Phoebe strictly as a helper, he might have chosen other Greek words which address this nuance more, such as βοηθὸς (helper) or ὑπηρέτην ("one who functions as a helper, freq. [frequently] in a subordinate capacity, *helper, assistant*"). [26] If the cognate verb προΐστημι ("direct," "preside") is utilized to determine a definition for προστάτις, then Paul may be trying "to characterize Phoebe as a 'leader' of the church." [27]

(idos, ή.) προστάτης "patron" "benefactor"
προϊστημι "direct" "preside"

Paul's references to Priscilla, Euodia, Syntyche, and Junia are important to this discussion as well. In 67% of the occurrences in the New Testament, Priscilla is listed previous to that of her husband. Dunn believes this indicates that "she was the more dominant of the two." [28] Priscilla and Aquila held a church in their home and are classified as συνεργούς with Paul. Συνεργούς denotes equality, coming from συν meaning "with" and εργόν meaning "work." Philippians 4.2-3 also identifies Euodia and Syntyche with συνήθλησάν (from συνήθλήέω, meaning "working together with"). Furnish writes that

Priscilla — Euodia — Syntyche — Junia

συνεργός, όν (n.s.m. adj.) — associate

> whenever Paul speaks of laboring 'in the gospel' [as the case here] he is speaking of his own apostolic ministry (Rom 1.9; II Cor 10.14) or of the ministry of his closest associates (of Timothy in I Thess 3.2 and of an unnamed brother—Apollos?—in II Cor 8.18). It is no insignificant thing for Euodia and Syntyche to be included in this company. [29]

laboring in the gospel

B. Ehrman comments that their discord is a concern of Paul "evidently because of their prominent standing in the community." [30] The reference in Rom 16.7 to Junia as "outstanding among the apostles" is most likely a reference to another significant woman in Paul's circle of ministry. [31]

Paul's identification of freedom in Christ as a key component of his gospel, then, has ramifications in the way he conducts his ministry, particularly in the significant role that women play. This result overlaps in some ways with the liberation of women as advocated in the Isis cult. As in Paul, this issue of freedom is not limited to women. Similarly, "One of the most highly-touted features of Isiacism was its theoretical equality of the sexes." [32]

Salvation - acutely dynamic act in which gods & humans snatch others by force from serious peril.

Salvation

Another concept in the Pauline letters that is stressed with considerable frequency is salvation. Paul uses σῴζω ("save") twenty-nine times (more than any other New Testament author), σωτήρ ("savior") twelve times or half of the occurrences in the New Testament, σωτηρία ("salvation") a total of eighteen times, σωτήριος ("salvation") one time, and σωτήριος ("salvation") also on one occurrence.[33] Another word ῥύομαι ("save, rescue") is utilized eleven times.[34] L. Morris concludes, "Such statistics show that Paul is interested in the concept of salvation, more so, indeed, than any other NT writer."[35]

While Christianity has fostered the idea that salvation is being "saved from sin," W. Foerster reflects that in the ancient Greek world, "σῴζω and σωτηρία mean first 'to save' and 'salvation' in the sense of an acutely dynamic act in which gods or men snatch others by force from serious peril."[36] The Isis cult views salvation from this perspective too.[37] W. Bauer comments on an inscription found in 1 BC detailing Isis's role in salvation, namely that she would save those who call upon her "in the hour of death."[38] This combines the appeal to Isis for deliverance and eternal life.

Salvation for Paul encompasses more than the salvation of souls. Morris elaborates upon the wider scope that

> salvation includes an ongoing triumph over the forces of evil. And Paul looks forward to the end of this age and sees salvation as having its effect throughout eternity. We should not think of salvation as simply negative, as 'deliverance from . . . ' It is that, but it is more. *It involves wholeness, wellness, health, goodness.* Thus Paul says that Christ "delivered us from the power of darkness," but immediately adds, "and transferred us into the kingdom of his beloved Son" (Col 1:13).[39]

Salvation can also be described encompassing both the present and the future, the "here and not yet." For instance, in 2 Cor 1.10, as Morris notes, Paul says "that Christ *has delivered* us 'from so great a death' and who *will deliver*, and adds that this is the one 'on whom we have set our hope that he *will still deliver.*' "[40] Dunn comments that two tenses of salvation exist for Paul: "the aorist and the continuous. These are grammatical signifiers of the two phases of salvation, the beginning and the ongoing."[41]

Paul also uses the idea of "call" in reference to salvation, such as in 2 Tim 1.9. This idea is also reflected in 2 Thess 2.13-14, "But we should always give thanks to God for you, brethren beloved by the Lord, because God has chosen you from the beginning for salvation through sanctification by the Spirit and faith in the truth. It was for this that He called you through your gospel." Salvation is never derived from the effort of humans, but "the initiative in salvation is with God" and "is brought about by God in Christ."[42]

Not all of Paul's uses of σῴζω are about salvation.[43] Variant definitions exist as noted by Bauer, such as "to preserve or rescue fr. [from] natural dangers and afflictions, *save, keep from harm, preserve, rescue*."[44]

In 1 Tim 2.15, Paul states, "But women will be preserved [σωθήσεται] *3ps f p ind.* through the bearing of children if they continue in faith and love and sanctity with self-restraint." Although some understand σωθήσεται in the sense of "saved,"[45] rendering it in the sense of "preserved" is preferable in the context.[46] The sentence in 1 Tim 2.15 is a third class conditional with the apodosis expressing a probable future. The effect of being preserved through childbirth will occur only if the condition in the protasis is met. Also, the phrase διὰ τῆς τεκνογονίας is often misunderstood as instrumental when it is more likely locative. Childbirth is not the means of salvation but the location of deliverance.[47]

Paul uses σῴζω without reference to Christian salvation in other places. In 1 Tim 4.16, he exhorts Timothy to protect himself from possible danger by practicing consistency between his words and his deeds. He says, "Pay close attention to yourself and to your teaching; persevere in these things, for as you do this you will preserve [σώσεις] both yourself from harm and those who hear you."[48] In 2 Tim 4.18, he refers to being safely delivered to the Lord's kingdom.

When Paul uses the noun σωτήρ, he often designates this to be either Christ or God. God is the referent in 1 Tim 1.1, 1 Tim 2.3, Titus 1.3, Titus 2.10, and Titus 3.4. However, on some occasions, no reference is given within the immediate surrounding context is given to "define" the word Savior. For this reason, it may be appropriate to render σωτήρ as "one who rescues."[49]

Concerning the use of σωτηρία, Paul generally utilizes this term to refer to salvation. However, Dunn writes that "the term [σωτηρία] would no doubt have been familiar to Paul's readers also in the everyday sense of 'bodily health, preservation.' "[50] Bauer renders "*deliverance, salvation*" as appropriate translations for σωτηρία.[51] Jesus is described as a deliverer who delivers people from their afflictions in life. Whether these afflictions be physical or mental, Christ is portrayed as a deliverer.[52] When one looks at the multitude of trials that Paul endured during his missionary journeys, it is not surprising for him to construct a theology of God as deliverer. In 2 Cor 1.3, Paul describes Christ as θεὸς πάσης παρακλήσεως, but παρακλήσεως can be defined as "lifting of another's spirits, *comfort, consolation*."[53] Therefore, God can be designated as the God of help in 2 Cor 1.3-7 in Paul's estimation. He continues to stress God as deliverer in 2 Thess 1.6-8. While these verses may address more physical discomfort from afflictions, Phil 4.6-7 sees God as one who brings peace to his followers, alleviating them from anxiety. Paul also testifies to the faithfulness of Christ in his own life, who is faithful to deliver him out of all his persecutions. This truth is evident from Paul's words

παράκλησις, εως, ἡ
προστάσις

in 2 Tim 3.10-12, "what persecutions I [Paul] endured, and out of them all the Lord rescued me!"

Paul's theology of salvation or deliverance is also informed by his use of the word ῥύομαι. This word is used eleven times by Paul in a variety of situations, as seen in table 4.2.

Paul has been delivered or expects to be delivered from a wide range of afflictions, ranging from disobedient people to the power of the darkness. He has also been delivered from trials, such as "a peril of death" (2 Cor 1.10a), the "lion's mouth" (2 Tim 4.17), and the "authority of the darkness"[54] (Col 1.13). In short, Paul testifies, "out of them [persecutions] all the Lord rescued me!" (2 Tim 3.11). Because of Paul's confidence in God's delivering acts, he trusts Him for deliverance from his present afflictions, signified by the aorist subjunctive (showing an act of prayer in these instances). Paul prays to be delivered from afflictions with others, such as disobedient people in Judea and perverse and evil men. He equates Christ as his ὁ ῥυόμενος.

In conclusion, Paul uses various words for salvation, deliverance, or preservation from harm. I have argued that Paul incorporates the idea of rescue or deliverance from danger in many instances as well as the future promise of eternal life. Similarly, in the Isis cult, salvation is both meant as eternal life as well as deliverance from earthly plights.

Baptism

Baptism is a theme that runs throughout Paul's epistles. Perhaps it is such a priority for Paul because this is one of the first things he is commanded to do after he receives his sight. Acts 22.16 reads, "Now why do you delay? Get up and be baptized, and wash away your sins, calling on His name." G. R. Beasley-Murray reasons, "Since Paul himself had received baptism, and had

Table 4.2.   Variant Uses and Tenses of ῥύομαι

Scripture	Peril Rescued From	Tense of ῥύομαι
Rom 7.24	Body of this death	Future
Rom 11.26	Rescuer/deliverer = Christ	Present
Rom 15.31	Disobedient people	Aorist subjunctive (prayer)
2 Cor 1.10a	A peril of death	Aorist
2 Cor 1.10b	Future afflictions	Future
2 Tim 3.11	All persecutions	Aorist
2 Tim 4.17	Lion's mouth	Aorist
2 Tim 4.18	Every evil deed	Future
Col 1.13	Power of the darkness	Aorist
1 Thess 1.10	Wrath to come	Present
2 Thess 3.2	Perverse and evil men	Aorist subjunctive (prayer)

reason to believe that all the other Christians were baptized, it is clear that the rite existed prior to his conversion."[55] This fact can be gathered due to the ministry of John the Baptist in baptizing others for repentance (Acts 19.4, Mk 1.4-8), "of Jesus (see Jn 3.25-26, 4.1-3), and of the apostles from the day of Pentecost on (Acts 2.37-41), and the missionary commission of the risen Lord, recorded in Matthew 28.19."[56] In short, Paul expects and "takes it for granted that all his readers (including those unknown to him personally) have been baptized."[57]

Romans 6.3-11 describes the Pauline language utilized in the baptismal process. It reads as follows,

> Or do you not know that all of us who have been baptized into Christ Jesus have been baptized into His death? Therefore we have been buried with Him through baptism into death, so that as Christ was raised from the dead through the glory of the Father, so we too might walk in newness of life. For if we have become united with Him in the likeness of His death, certainly we shall also be in the likeness of His resurrection, knowing this, that our old self was crucified with Him, in order that our body of sin might be done away with, so that we would no longer be slaves to sin; for he who has died is freed from sin. Now if we have died with Christ, we believe that we shall also live with Him, knowing that Christ, having been raised from the dead, is never to die again; death no longer is master over Him. For the death that He died, He died to sin once for all; but the life that He lives, He lives to God. Even so consider yourselves to be dead to sin, but alive to God in Christ Jesus.

A. Schweitzer comments, "Baptism is for him [Paul] a being buried and rising again, because it takes place in the name of Jesus Christ, who was buried and rose again."[58] Dunn agrees, "It is hardly forcing the sense to see the two phrases as equivalent: 'baptized into his death' = 'buried with him through baptism into death.' In other words, the 'into Christ' of participation in Christ was effected 'through baptism.' "[59] Perhaps it can be gathered that Christians are being assimilated with Christ since they are united with Him.

Dunn also expresses his curiosity of baptism, saying,

> is the phrase 'baptized into Christ' a shortened version of 'baptized into the name of Christ'? Do metaphors like 'washed,' 'sealed,' and 'put off/put on clothes' reflect aspects of baptismal ceremony already at the time of Paul? In the light of the conclusions already reached a positive response to both questions has a great degree of plausibility.[60]

Concerning correspondence to the Isis cult, baptism is used as a means of initiation. This fact has been discussed at length in chapter three. However, the link that appears stronger than baptism is the fact of the conversion experience. Dunn notes that baptism is part of the conversion experience in

Pauline Christianity because conversion does not consist of "some private spiritual transaction."[61] Rather, the act of baptism is a public event and most likely includes a public confession as seen in Rom 10.9, "that if you confess with your mouth Jesus as Lord, and believe in your heart that God raised Him from the dead, you will be saved."[62]

Baptism is seen as a sign of conversion. Concerning the conversion experience in the Isis cult, Dunn concludes, "There is indeed an almost inevitable similarity between experiences of radical conversion, such as that of Lucius and that of Paul, and language of death and life is a natural expression of such experiences."[63] Koester agrees with Dunn, "One should not deny that the New Testament and the mysteries often speak the same language. When Paul says that those who have been baptized have died with Christ and should, therefore, walk in a new life, his words closely resemble those of the initiation into the Isis mysteries."[64] Dunn cites Rom 6.4 as addressing this concept.[65] It reads, "Therefore, we have been buried with Him through baptism into death, so that as Christ was raised from the dead, through the glory of the Father, *so we too might walk in newness of life.*"[66] Baptism in Pauline Christianity "constituted almost literally a 'rite of passage.' Those baptized were thereby renouncing old ways of life and committing themselves to a new way of life."[67] Beasley-Murray concludes, "This appeal [of "life consonant with participation in the redemption of Christ that lies in the heart of baptism"] is most extensively developed in Col 2.20–3.13. Therein lies the fact that the believer died and rose to Christ is not only a motive for Christ-like living, but a basis to work out the baptismal pattern of dying to sin and rising to righteousness."[68] Based upon these verses G. Bornkamm affirms that for Paul, "baptism is the appropriation of the new life, and the new life is the appropriation of baptism."[69]

Resurrection

Resurrection is also a concept that runs throughout Paul's epistles. L. J. Kreitzer assesses the terminology employed in discussing the resurrection. He says,

> The word *anistēmi* ("raise up") is used a total of five times with reference to the resurrection, both of Christ (1 Thess 4.14; cf. Rom 15.12) and of the believer (1 Thess 4.16; Eph 5.14). The verb *egeirō* ("raise," "cause to rise") appears a total of thirty-eight times with reference to the resurrection . . . and the compound verb *exegeirō* ("raise up") once in reference to the resurrection of believers (1 Cor 6.14). In addition the noun *anastasis* ("resurrection") is used eight times (Rom 1.4; 6.4; 1 Cor 15.12, 13, 21, 42; Phil 3.10; 2 Tim 2.18) and the noun *exanastasis* ("resurrection") occurs once (Phil 3.11). These terms are used of both the resurrection of Jesus Christ himself and the raising of the believers which the Lord's resurrection guarantees.[70]

Paul considers resurrection to be an integral part of his theology and focuses upon it in 1 Corinthians 15.[71] He also speaks of being with Christ in His resurrection, particularly in Rom 6.5, "For if we have become united with Him in the likeness of His death, certainly we shall also be in the likeness of His resurrection." This is reiterated in Rom 6.8, "Now if we have died with Christ, we believe that we shall also live with Him."

The same spirit that raises Christ from the dead is present in believers. Paul speaks of this in Rom 8.11, "But if the Spirit who raised Christ Jesus from the dead dwells in you, He who raised Christ Jesus from the dead will also give life to your mortal bodies through His spirit who dwells in you." It might be gathered that this verse touches on assimilation with Christ. This idea is alluded to in 2 Cor 4.14, "knowing that He who raised the Lord Jesus will raise us also with Jesus and will present us with you." But this concept of assimilation or union with Christ is quite clear in Eph 2.4-6 as follows:

> But God, being rich in mercy, because of His great love with which He loved us, even when we were dead in our transgressions, made us alive together with Christ (by grace you have been saved), and raised us with Him, and seated us with Him in the heavenly places, in Christ Jesus.

The resurrection which is achieved by the individual, from Paul's perspective, is directly linked to knowing Christ, as expressed in Phil 3.10: "that I may know Him and the power of His resurrection and the fellowship of His sufferings, being conformed to His death." Paul hopes, signaled by εἴ πως ("if in some way"), he may achieve this desired resurrection. Some translations (such as the NASB), classify εἴ πως as more of a purpose clause. In this manner, εἴ πως is seen to function as ἵνα. Exegetically speaking, the significance of seeing εἴ πως as ἵνα is to see the resurrection that Paul hopes to achieve as more of a factual reality, rather than a contingent element.

The resurrection is "the central motif in Paul's eschatology insofar as it inaugurates the age to come and provides the basis for future hope."[72] What is rather interesting is how Paul expresses this concept in the Greek. For example, Phil 3.11 uses the terminology, "τὴν ἐξανάστασιν τὴν ἐκ νεκρῶν." This is generally translated as "resurrection from the dead." However, as Kreitzer notes, "The Greek expression [in Phil 3.11] contains a much more dynamic image, conjuring up a picture of 'the standing up from the midst of corpses,' and lending weight to the somatic nature of the resurrection body."[73]

Other Concepts

Comparing more concepts present in Pauline Christianity with those of the Isis cult can be done efficiently in table 4.3.

Table 4.3.   Parallels in Pauline Christianity and the Isis Cult[74]

Pauline Scriptures	Concept	Isis Cult
People who accept Christ become new and put on the new self. See 2 Cor 5.17, Eph 4.22-24, Col 3.9-10.	New life/self	Lucius, an initiate of Isis, is transformed from a donkey into a human. Also, initiates of Isis are enabled to be reborn and are said to be placed on the path of "renewed life."
Resurrection is a core concept in Pauline theology. See (Acts 17.3, Acts 17.18, Acts 23.6, Acts 24.21, Acts 26.23), Rom 7.4, Rom 8.11, 1 Cor 6.14, 1 Cor 15.3-4, 1 Cor 15.12-13, 1 Cor 15.15-17, 1 Cor 15.20-22, 1 Cor 15.35-38, 1 Cor 15.42-49, 2 Cor 4.14-15, Gal 1.1, Eph 1.20, Eph 2.4-6, Col 2.12-13, 1 Thess 4.14.	Resurrection/ being raised	Isis is believed to raise Osiris from the dead. Thus, Osiris is classified as the resurrected god.
The concept of mystery is utilized in Pauline theology. See Rom 11.25, Rom 16.25-26, 1 Cor 2.7-10, 1 Cor 2.12-13, 1 Cor 4.1, 1 Cor 15.51, 2 Cor 4.3-4, 2 Cor 12.2-4, Eph 1.8-9, Eph 1.17, Eph 3.3-5, Eph 3.9-10, Col 1.26-29, Col 2.2-3, Col 4.3, 2 Thess 2.7.	Mystery	The Isis cult is a mystery religion and initiates can be entrusted with the secrets or mysteries of the cult.
The idea of being chosen or initiation language is apparent in Pauline theology. See Rom 8.29, Rom 9.15-18, Rom 9.27, Rom 11.5-6, Eph 1.4-5, Eph 1.11, Eph 3.3-5, 2 Tim 2.10-13.	Initiate and initiation language/ "predestination"	Isis encourages Lucius in dreams to become an initiate into her cult. The priest has to receive orders from Isis to allow the followers of Isis to undergo initiation.
The idea of salvation is a thread that runs through Pauline theology. See (Acts 4.12), Rom 10.9-10, Rom 10.13, Rom 11.11, Rom 13.11, 1 Thess 5.9, 1 Tim 2.4, 2 Tim 2.10, 2 Tim 3.15.	Salvation	Isis bestows salvation upon her initiates.
The Lord or God is identified as Savior by Paul. See Phil 3.20, 1 Tim 4.10, 2 Tim 1.10.	Savior	Isis is called the "holy and eternal saviour" of humankind."
God is merciful to humankind. See Rom 2.4, Rom 8.38-39, Eph 2.4-9, Eph 5.2, Titus 3.4-5.	Mercy	Isis is known for her kindness to individuals. She is described as the "altar of Mercy."

Pauline Scriptures	Concept	Isis Cult
The concept of light is evident in Pauline Christianity. See (Acts 13.47, Acts 22.6, Acts 26.23), 2 Cor 4.3-4, 2 Cor 4.6, 2 Cor 6.14, Eph 3.9-10, Eph 5.8-9, Eph 5.11, Eph 5.13-14, Phil 2.15, Col 1.12-13, 1 Thess 5.5, 1 Tim 6.16, (1 John 1.5, 1 John 1.7).	Light	Light is used in the festivals of Isis, in the initiation process, and Isis is honored with light. Isis is also believed to be the one who provides light to the stars.
Christians share the Lord's Supper and break bread together, which can be classified as communal meals. See (Acts 2.42, Acts 2.46), 1 Cor 10.16-17, 1 Cor 11.23-34.	Communal meal	After Lucius's birth into the mysteries, he celebrates with a banquet, party, and a "sacred breakfast."
Paul speaks of knowing Christ and being found in Christ. See Phil 3.8-10.	Relationship with Christ (or Isis)	Initiates of Isis enter into a relationship with her which might be seen to parallel the relationship Lucius has with Isis.
Believers in Christ are classified as sons, heirs, and children. See Rom 8.14-17, Rom 8.19-20, Rom 8.23, Rom 9.25-26, Gal 3.29, Gal 4.5-7, Eph 1.4-5, Eph 5.1, Col 1.12, 1 Thess 2.11.	Familial relationship	Those in the Isis cult are seen as initiates and possess a common bond, especially in comparison with those who are not initiated.
Paul (along with Silvanus and Timothy) describes his care as a mother in his relationship with the Thessalonians. See 1 Thess 2.7-8.	Mother	Isis is seen as mother of all. She demonstrates the tender loving care of a mother relating to the problems of humankind.
Paul is an advocate of freedom and equality in Christ. See Rom 10.12, 1 Cor 12.12-16, 2 Cor 3.17, Gal 2.4, Gal 3.28, Col 3.10-11.	Freedom/liberation/ equality	Isis is known for equality between men and women as well as providing liberation.
Paul uses many references of the identity of the believer in Christ or with Christ. See (Acts 17.28), 1 Cor 6.17, Gal 2.20, Eph 1.7-8, Eph 1.10-11, Eph 2.5-6, 2 Cor 5.17, Col 2.6-7, Col 2.9-13, Col 2.20, Col 3.11, 1 Thess 5.10, 2 Thess 1.12.	Identity one in/with Christ	In mystery religions, such as the Isis cult, the devotee is believed to become one with the deity.
In Pauline Christianity, believers belong to God and exist for Him. See 1 Cor 3.23, 1 Cor 6.19-20, 1 Cor 8.6.	Belonging to God/Isis	Lucius, the initiate of Isis, owes all his remaining time on earth to Isis because of the miracle she performs for him.

Pauline Scriptures	Concept	Isis Cult
The Lord is described as the source of help, comfort, peace, and relief for the Christian believer. See 2 Cor 1.3-7, 2 Cor 1.10, 2 Tim 3.11, 2 Tim 4.17-18, Phil 4.6-7, Col 1.13, 1 Thess 1.10, 2 Thess 1.6-8.	Source of help	Isis helps all who call upon her. Lucius is transformed from a donkey to a human because of Isis. She protects land-dwellers and sea-farers and drives away the woes of life.
Paul performs miracles throughout his ministry. See (Acts 14.8-10, Acts 19.11-12, Acts 20.9-12).	Miracles	Isis is believed to perform "miracles" because of her magical powers.
Christianity is not an accepted religion from the onset; consider the persecution that the Christians endured during the first century under Nero and Domitian. See (Acts 17.6-8).	Not accepted by the Roman government	The Isis cult has laws issued against it, especially during the reign of Augustus.
Eternal life is given to believers from the Lord. See Rom 5.21, 1 Cor 2.9, Gal 3.29, 2 Tim 1.10, 2 Tim 2.11-13.	Eternal life	Initiates of the Isis cult are believed to inherit eternal life.
Christ dies, and believers also die with Christ. See Rom 5.6, Rom 5.9, Rom 5.10, Gal 2.20, Col 2.20, Col 3.3, 1 Thess 4.14, and 2 Tim 2.11-13.	Dying	The myth of Isis involves Osiris dying and Isis raising him back to life. Also, initiation into the Isis cult is performed in the practice of "voluntary death."
Paul draws a distinction between the things on earth and the things in heaven. See Phil 3.19-20, Col 3.1-4.	Differentiation between things on earth and things above	The differentiation between the things of the earth and the things above reflect mystic language.
As a follower of Christ, Paul experiences persecution. See 2 Tim 3.10-12.	Persecution	Followers of Isis experience persecution, but would rather be martyred than abandon their devotion to her.
Paul opposes demonic powers and anything or anyone that clashes with his teaching. The magical powers that Isis exhibit could be problematic from the Pauline perspective. See (Acts 16.16, Acts 19.19, Acts 19.23-41), Col 2.8, Col 2.23, 1 Tim 1.3-4, 1 Tim 1.6-7, 1 Tim 4.7, 1 Tim 6.20-21, 2 Tim 3.13, 2 Tim 4.15.	Clash with cults/demons/etc.	Isis is a sorceress or goddess of magic. Her son, Horus, is known as the "son of an enchantress." Spells of Isis from Egypt have also been documented and preserved. Isis is also believed to bestow her healing powers upon those who visited her temple.

Pauline Scriptures	Concept	Isis Cult
Baptism signifies conversion in Pauline Christianity. See Acts 19.4-5, Acts 22.16, Rom 6.3-11, 1 Cor 6.1, Col 2.12-13, Titus 3.4.	Baptism	Baptism is practiced in the Isis cult as an act of initiation.
Paul advocates prayer for believers in Christ. See Phil 4.6, 1 Thess 5.17.	Prayer	People pray to Isis for answers to their plights in life.
Self-control or self-mastery is a common topic for Paul. See (Acts 24.25), Rom 2.17-24, Rom 6.12-13, Rom 7.5, Rom 13.13, 1 Cor 5.1, 1 Cor 5.9, 1 Cor 6.13, 1 Cor 6.15-16, 1 Cor 6.18, 1 Cor 6.20, 1 Cor 7.9, 1 Cor 9.24-27, 1 Cor 12.21, Gal 5.16, Gal 5.24, Eph 2.3, Eph 4.19, Eph 4.22-24, Eph 5.3, Eph 5.5, Col 2.23, Col 3.5, Cor 12.21, 1 Thess 4.3-5, 1 Thess 4.7, 2 Tim 2.19, 2 Tim 2.22, Titus 1.7-8, Titus 2.11-12, Titus 2.14, Titus 3.3.	Self-control/self-mastery	In initiation into the Isis cult, Lucius is to regulate his diet by abstaining from certain foods. Following his bath, Lucius is given further dietary instructions and is obligated to be celibate.
Believers in Christ are servants and live for the Lord. See Rom 14.7-8, 2 Cor 4.5, 2 Cor 6.4, 2 Cor 11.23, Eph 4.12, Phil 1.1, Col 4.12, 1 Tim 4.6.	Service/slavery	Following initiation, Lucius is required to tell of his deliverance to others. He also devotes himself to the worship of Isis and serves her as a lay person.
God is the source of all existence. See (Acts 17.24-26, Acts 17.28), Rom 11.36, 1 Cor 8.6, 1 Cor 10.26, Col 1.16-20.	Source	Isis is described as the source of the elements as well as "mother of the universe" among other titles. She is thought to give light to the sun and the universe as well as rotating the earth.
Paul experiences many trials for the faith, but is confident that Christ will deliver him as well as believers in Christ. See (Acts 14.22, Acts 20.19), Rom 8.18, Rom 12.12, Phil 1.29-30, 1 Cor 1.3-7, 1 Cor 4.11-13, 2 Cor 4.17, 2 Cor 4.8-12, 2 Cor 6.4-6, 2 Cor 11.23-28, 1 Thess 3.3-4, 1 Thess 3.7, 2 Thess 1.4-6, 2 Tim 1.8, 2 Tim 1.12, 2 Tim 2.3-7, 2 Tim 2.8-10, 2 Tim 3.11-12, 2 Tim 4.5.	Suffering/trials	Consider the plight of Lucius as a donkey. Also, people struggling with their plights in life call upon Isis for deliverance. (They may have been equally able to relate to Paul's words.)

Pauline Scriptures	Concept	Isis Cult
People who believe in Jesus are His followers. See Rom 13.13.	Believing	Those who believe in Isis can be described as her followers.
Paul speaks against regulations imposed upon food. See Col 2.20-23, 1 Tim 4.3-5.	Regulations imposed upon food	Lucius observes special dietary regulations in his initiation into the Isis cult and Osiris cult.
Paul himself experiences visions and falls into a trance. See (Acts 22.17), 2 Cor 12.1-4, Col 2.18-19.	Trance/visions	Isis speaks to Lucius through dreams. In this state, she reveals herself to him and directs his steps.
Unity is a part of the Christian experience. See (Acts 2.42, Acts 2.44-46), 1 Cor 12.12, Eph 4.3-4, Phil 2.1-4, Col 3.14-15, 1 Thess 5.13, 1 Thess 5.15.	Unity	The initiates of Isis can be described as a cohesive group as they partake in activities and festivals together. The initiated also celebrate with a banquet, party, and a breakfast.
Paul is to be a witness for Christ following his conversion. See (Acts 26.15-16).	Witness	Lucius is required to be a witness for Isis after his initiation.

Concepts in the Isis cult have also compared and contrasted with Christianity (not specifically Pauline) on numerous levels. These have been classified in table 4.4.

As table 4.4 illustrates, many commonalities can be found between Isis and Christianity. For instance, Isis offers "purification, forgiveness, communion, regeneration, and immortality of soul" to her faithful devotees.[99] Christ also offers forgiveness and purification of sins as stated in 1 John 1.9: "If we confess our sins, He is faithful and righteous to forgive us our sins and to

Table 4.4.   Similarities Between Isis and Christianity

Isis	Concept	Christianity
"Purification, forgiveness, communion, regeneration, and immortality of soul" are all "rewards which she [Isis] could offer the faithful initiate."	Forgiveness of sins/ purification	1 John 1.9–"If we confess our sins, He is faithful and righteous to forgive us our sins and to cleanse us from all unrighteousness."
"The gates of Hell, besides salvation were in her [Isis's] hands" as well as offering "immortality of soul" to her faithful devotees.	Salvation	John 3.16–"For God so loved the world, that He gave His only begotten Son, that whoever believes in Him shall not perish, but have eternal life."

Isis	Concept	Christianity
"Isis helped anyone who called upon her, both women and men, in any area of trouble, from childbirth to shipwreck."	Delivering people from their plights on earth	The plethora of accounts of deliverance are attested to throughout the pages of the OT and NT, ranging anywhere from the deliverance of the Israelites from Egypt in Exod 14 to Peter's deliverance from jail in Acts 12.
The Kyme Aretalogy states, "I [Isis] divided the earth from the heaven."	Dividing earth from heaven	Gen 1.7-9–"God made the expanse, and separated the waters which were below the expanse from the waters which were above the expanse; and it was so. God called the expanse heaven. . . . Then God said, 'Let the waters below the heavens be gathered into one place, and let the dry land appear': and it was so. God called the dry land earth."
The Kyme Aretalogy reads, "I [Isis] showed the paths of the stars. I ordered the course of the sun and the moon."	Control over the sun and moon	1) Jer 31.35– "Thus says the Lord, who gives the sun for light by day and the fixed order of the moon and the stars for light by night." 2) Ps 104.19–"He [the Lord] made the moon for the seasons; the sun knows the place of its setting."
1) The Kyme Aretalogy asserts, "I [Isis] am the Queen of rivers and winds and sea. . . . I am the Queen of the thunderbolt. I stir up the sea and I calm it. . . . I am the Queen of seamanship. I make the navigable unnavigable when it pleases me." 2) P. Oxy. XI.1380 describes Isis as "guardian and guide and seas, and Lady of the mouths and rivers."	Control over bodies of water	1) Isa 51.15– "Thus says the Lord . . . who stirs up the sea so that its waves roar; the Lord of hosts is His name." 2) Consider the Lord's acts on the Sea of Galilee in stilling the storm as evident in the gospel accounts, such as Mark 4.35-41.
Isis is responsible for healing those who went to her temple as well as the "art of medicine."	Healing physical ailments	The gospel accounts describe the power of Jesus healing people, ranging from the demoniacs to the blind.

Isis	*Concept*	*Christianity*
The Kyme Aretalogy reads, "I [Isis] overcome Fate. Fate harkens to me." Also, the Kyme Aretalogy reads, "Whatever I [Isis] please, this too shall come to an end."	Control over fate	Ps 103.19–"The Lord has established His throne in the heavens, and His sovereignty rules over all."

cleanse us from all unrighteousness." Besides forgiveness, Christ, as well as Isis, offers salvation. Witt writes, "She [Isis] resurrected. The gates of Hell, besides salvation were in her hands."[100] Furthermore, "the second-century novelist Apuleius of Madaura calls Isis 'mother' and 'holy and eternal savior' (*sospitatrix*) of the human race (*Metamorphoses* 11.15-35)."[101] The offer of salvation in Christianity is evident in John 3.16: "For God so loved the world, that He gave His only begotten Son, that whoever believes in Him shall not perish, but have eternal life."

Even in the formation of the world, Isis had a role. Isis is credited for dividing the earth from the heavens; however, in Christianity, God is known for this act. Gen 1.7-8 reads, "God made the expanse, and separated the waters which were below the expanse from the waters which were above the expanse; and it was so. God called the expanse heaven." This act "shared" by both God and Isis (as well as other shared acts and concepts) may have caused perplexity among people concerning Christianity and the tenets of the Isis cult.

Furthermore, Isis helped in people's earthly lives just as God intervened in the troubles of humanity. LiDonnici says, "Isis helped anyone who called upon her, both women and men, in any area of trouble, from childbirth to shipwreck."[102] God also delivers people from their troubles as attested to in the pages of the Old Testament and New Testament. Whether it was the woes of the Israelites in the wilderness or the healing of a leper, God intervenes directly in human affairs.

Isis is also known to have power over fate. The Kyme Aretalogy speaks of the words of Isis, saying, "I [Isis] overcome Fate. Fate harkens to me."[103] However, this can be contrasted with God's sovereign control as evident in the biblical text. The "dominance" of Isis is overshadowed by the works of God as recorded in Scripture.

It is also interesting that just as God is no respecter of persons, Isis also does not show favoritism. Witt writes of the similarities between the two, saying that "the Pauline and the Isiac faith had at least one common characteristic," which can be described as putting "aside racial and social distinctions."[104]

Besides being an advocate for equality, another similarity between Isis and Christ is the power over the seas. Isis is known for her control over the seas, saying, "I [Isis] am the Queen of rivers and winds and sea. . . . I am the Queen of the thunderbolt. I stir up the sea and I calm it. . . . I am the Queen of seamanship. I make the navigable unnavigable when it pleases me."[105]

However, in the gospel stories, Christ is known for exercising dominance over bodies of water. For instance, Jesus takes authority over the wind and the waves in the Sea of Galilee. In doing so, He may have been demonstrating His dominance over pagan gods and goddesses who are invoked by the people.[106]

Furthermore, Isis is credited for healing those who go to her temple, and she is also responsible for the "art of medicine."[107] On a contrasting note, a multitude of accounts in the gospel accounts exist where Jesus heals the less fortunate. These range from demoniacs to the crippled. Jesus even raises the dead. Just as Christ intervenes in the plights of humanity, Isis is believed to provide assistance as well.

In conclusion, in light of the qualities held by Isis, ranging from magic to salvation, her appeal is vast in the ancient world. Her power may be labeled as "limitless." She protects the sailors, cares for the dead, has the power to intervene in people's plights during their earthly lives, and exercises power over fate. Christianity also touches on a lot of these concepts, which may have fostered connection between the two belief systems or created conflict. However, in contrast to Christianity, Isis holds a special place in the hearts of women, due to the fact that Isis is a feminine goddess and shares many experiences that women may undergo throughout the course of their lifetimes. Christianity also holds widespread appeal among its followers.

PAULINE CONTRASTS WITH THE ISIS CULT

Different Isiac Practices

While both Pauline Christianity and the Isis cult have a number of notable features in common, this does not mean that the two religions are identical in their practices. Some concepts contain stronger parallels than others. For example, the issue of freedom prevalent in the Isis cult is focused more along gender lines. That is, the Isis cult is more concerned with the equality and liberation of women. In comparison with Pauline Christianity, Paul cuts across ethnic barriers to erase the Jew/Gentile distinction, thus liberating different ethnic groups. The book of Romans caters to this theme as expressed in Rom 10.12, "there is no distinction between Jew and Greek." But this fact is also attested in Col 3.10-11 and Gal 3.28.

Concerning salvation, both the Isis cult and Pauline Christianity hold the promise of eternal life for their followers. Similarities are also seen in the "salvation language" such as classifying salvation as deliverance. However, this is not to imply that these two practices are equivalent on all levels. While the Isis cult does offer eternal life to her devotees, a price is to be paid for initiation into the Isis cult. It is highly unlikely that all classes of people can afford such a price to "secure" salvation. However, in Pauline Christianity, Paul makes it clear that no such cost is required to receive salvation and cautions against attempting to earn salvation. This caution is seen in Eph 2.8-9, "For by grace you have been saved through faith; and that not of yourselves, it is the gift of God; not as a result of works, so that no one may boast." The Isis cult's view of salvation may be deemed as "works-related," due to the monetary fee, but also because the initiate is to undergo dietary regulations and pursue a life of celibacy. If Lucius is faithful and obedient in his worship, celibacy, and devotion to the goddess, he is promised to have his fate extended.[108] While this appears to be solely in reference to Lucius's earthly life, perhaps a discussion can be raised as to his "eternal" life.

Differences also can be accounted for in the practice of baptism. Both Pauline Christianity and the Isis cult practice baptism, but is that enough to draw a solid parallel? Several differences may be considered. First, baptism in the initiation account of Lucius does not occur at the temple, but at the baths. However, it is in the presence of initiates of Isis just as baptism is in the presence of believers in the faith. Lucius utters no verbal affirmation at his baptism nor is he baptized "in the name of Isis." In contrast, early Christians are baptized into Jesus just as they confess "Jesus as Lord." Dunn writes that baptism into Christ is "effected 'through baptism.' "[109] Galatians 3.27 says, "For all of you who were baptized into Christ have clothed yourselves with Christ."

Other regulations and rituals are observed by an initiate into the Isis cult besides baptism, as is expressed in the account by Apuleius. This includes three episodes involving water rather than just one, as in Christianity. Before Lucius even calls upon the goddess Isis, he purifies himself in the sea, dunking his head underneath the water a total of seven times since seven is proper for "religious rituals."[110] He then prays for rest from the cruelties in life. The second episode is the act of Lucius using sea spray to sprinkle himself. It is recorded that Lucius is awestruck with the presence of Isis and sprinkles himself with "sea-spray."[111] The third episode of water includes the bath and sprinkling.[112] Apuleius writes of Lucius's experience, "When I [Lucius] had taken the customary bath, he [the priest] began by asking the gods' favor and then cleansed me with purificatory sprinkling."[113]

Concerning the idea of resurrection, Pauline Christianity and the Isis cult share similar language.[114] Lucius is seen as reborn in his Isiac initiation (and later his Osirian initiation). In a similar fashion, Paul writes in Rom 6.4, "Therefore, we have been buried though baptism into death, so that as Christ was raised from the dead, through the glory of the Father, so we too might walk in newness of life." The difference between the Isis cult and Christianity is how deeply resurrection is integrated into its message. For Isis, resurrection is seen more in a symbolic form. Romans 6.5 says, "For if we have become united with Him in the likeness of his death, certainly we shall also be in the likeness of His resurrection."

"Inequality" of Women

At first reading of the Pauline epistles, one might conclude that Paul does not esteem women equally to men. C. S. Keener says, "No NT writer has been more criticized for his allegedly negative portrayal of women than the apostle Paul."[115] V. P. Furnish adds, "The apostle Paul has the unenviable distinction of having been and remaining one of history's most controversial and misunderstood figures."[116] This is certainly true with regard to his view on women. Statements like "woman is the glory of man" (1 Cor 11.7), or that "woman [is created] for man's sake" (1 Cor 11.9), help to foster the idea that women are created solely for the benefit of man. When coupled with household codes, stating that the wife is to be subject to her husband (Eph 5.24, 1 Tim 2.12, Col 3.18, Titus 2.5), it is no wonder people label Paul as a "misogynist."

Paul should not be labeled the "bad guy" he is made out to be. However, Paul's restrictions might not necessarily reflect the patriarchal norm of Roman society, where the *paterfamilias* was the head of the household. Paul could be responding to the "enthusiastic enactment of the Pauline equality preserved in Gal 3:28."[117] Ehrman suggests that because of Gal 3.28, some believed that all have "equal standing in Christ" and have "begun to urge a radical egalitarian form of community" where slaves and masters are equal with one another, as well as men and women.[118] The household codes are "intended to put a halt to this way of thinking."[119]

In any case the liberation of women in the Isis cult appears to be unrestricted, while in Pauline Christianity, however freeing, limits are imposed. The contrast here is in the extent to which social freedom from women is enacted. In terms of the Isis cult, the liberation of women may have been an attractive feature in contrast to the subservience of women which is advocated by Paul, as well as the clash with the order that is imposed by Roman society. If those who hear the liberating message of Gal 3.28 are freed from their ethnic and gender differences, actually causing an "unrest in Christian communities,"[120] the liberation that the Isis cult offers might also be welcome in the ears of many. While Paul does attempt to hamper the initial emancipating impact of Gal 3.28 in subsequent letters by the introduction of socially restrictive household codes, the same cannot be said of the Isis cult. While some may dispute the dates and authorship of Ephesians, Colossians, 1 Timothy and Titus, there is no disputing that they are written after Galatians and that they do contain such codes (Eph 5.22-33, Col 3.18-4.1, 1 Tim 2.1-15, 5.1-2, 6.1-2, 6.17-19, Titus 2.1-3.8).

CONCLUSION

While it is true that no one would mistake Pauline Christianity for the Isis cult, their similarities suggest that they may well have appealed to the same kind of person. The lure of new concepts such as freedom, salvation, baptism, and resurrection would have been powerful, especially to people outside of the ruling classes. Freedman, slaves, and women may have been attracted to both Isis and Christianity. Indeed, they may have sampled both before settling on one of them; or, they may have moved back and forth between the two.[121]

Pauline Christianity appeals to those who are hoping to feel a significant part of a community, being attracted to thoughts like those in 1 Cor 12.12: "For even as the body is one and yet has many members, and all the members of the body, though they are many, are one body, so also is Christ." Or Paul's exhortation in Phil 2.3-4: "Do nothing from selfishness or empty conceit, but with humility of mind regard one another as more important than yourselves; do not merely look out for your own personal interests, but also for the interests of others."[122]

Isis appeals heavily to women but also to men. Some of the trials that she experiences are common ground in identifying with women, such as the death of her husband or the bearing of her child. M. D. Donalson writes that Isis is "an ideal model and patroness for parenting, the model par excellence for married life, safety in childbirth, strength in sorrow."[123] However, this is not to say that men feel excluded from the cult.[124] Rather, the initiation in *Metamorphoses* does not describe a woman being initiated, but a man named Lucius. Men are also priests in the Isis cult.

Just as men take leadership roles in the Isis cult, men also find fulfillment in Christianity. Consider the example of the twelve apostles or the fact that all New Testament books with known authorship are traced to men. However, women are also attracted to Christianity, such as Paul's list of commendable women in Rom 16 (Phoebe, Junia, Priscilla, Junia, Mary, Tryphaena, Tryphosa, and Persis). Household codes directed to slaves and masters (Eph 6.5-9, Col 3.22-4.1, 1 Tim 6.1-2) plus Paul's letter to a slave owner (Philemon) suggests that slaves are also attracted to Christianity.

Thus, Pauline Christianity and the Isis cult, though worlds apart from the modern perspective, may not have seemed so different to a person struggling to find meaning and hope in the difficult environment of the Roman empire. Christianity, the newest "cult" may well have drawn people from the more established Isis cult or been seen as a new alternative. We will look to 1 Timothy in the next chapter to see how this perspective may have surfaced in the New Testament.

NOTES

1. J. D. G. Dunn, *Christian Liberty: A New Testament Perspective* (Grand Rapids: Eerdmans, 1993), 3.
2. J. K. Chamblin, "Freedom/Liberty," *DPL*, 313, emphasis added.
3. J. D. G. Dunn, *The Theology of Paul the Apostle* (Grand Rapids: Eerdmans, 1998), 328.
4. J. M. Everts, "Conversion and Call of Paul," *DPL*, 161.
5. Dunn, *Theology of Paul*, 320.
6. Dunn, *Theology of Paul*, 346-47.
7. All Scripture verses will be taken from the NASB unless otherwise indicated.
8. This can be drawn from κατα + δουλόω. Καταδουλόω can be defined as *"enslave, reduce to slavery"* (Bauer, "διάκονος," BDAG, 230). The only New Testament uses of καταδουλόω can both be attributed to Paul; the other occurrence is in 2 Cor 11.20.
9. Dunn, *Theology of Paul*, 346.
10. Dunn, *Theology of Paul*, 388.
11. R. N. Longenecker, *Paul: Apostle of Liberty* (New York: Harper & Row, 1964), 105.
12. The choice of ἀλλὰ here is significant for ἀλλα carries a higher semantic weight than δὲ and Paul is using it to stress the magnitude of his message of the grace of God. While δὲ is used when contrast is "scarcely discernable" (Bauer, "δὲ," BDAG, 213), the adversative particle ἀλλὰ, denotes opposition (from the Latin *adversari*, to oppose), which indicates a "difference with or contrast to what precedes" (Bauer, "ἀλλὰ," BDAG, 44). The etymology of ἀλλὰ may explain this nuance for ἀλλὰ originates from the neuter plural form of ἄλλος, meaning "otherwise" (Bauer, "ἀλλὰ," 44). In summary, the variance that δὲ exhibits as a coordinating conjunction is trite as evident by the definitions of "and" as well as "but" in comparison to ἀλλὰ solely being used to distinguish contrast.
13. Emphasis added.
14. S. T. Foh, "A Male Leadership View: The Head of the Woman is the Man," in *Women in Ministry: Four Views* (ed. Bonnidell Clouse & Robert G. Clouse; Downers Grove: InterVarsity 1989), 88.
15. Beasley-Murray, "Baptism," 63.
16. The verb form of διάκονος, διακονέω, is used in Rom 15.25 to describe Paul's ministry.
17. B. J. Dodd, *Problem with Paul* (Downer's Grove: InterVarsity Press, 1996), 23.
18. Dodd, *Problem with Paul*, 23.
19. See NASB, NIV, ASV, NKJV.
20. Bauer, "διάκονος," BDAG, 230. While I normally would hesitate to employ a double entendre for word studies, this case is an exception. A double entendre for Phoebe's role is also affirmed by B. D. Ehrman, *The New Testament: A Historical Introduction to the Early Christian Writings* (3d ed.; Oxford: Oxford University Press, 2004), 396.

21. In the ancient world, letters did not always reach their destination point. C. Roetzel elaborates on this phenomenon, saying that, no such [postal] delivery network was available for private correspondence. And, while the wealthy could afford couriers, either slaves or trusted employees, to deliver letters, the great majority of the population had to content itself with less reliable means. They turned to a traveling businessman, a friend on a journey, a total stranger or even a camel or donkey driver willing to promise delivery for a fee. Such ad hoc arrangements were often unreliable, and the cost of delivery worked a hardship on the sender. *We do not know what percentage of the letters was stolen and read, was undeliverable, or was simply discarded.* We are aware that senders were often anxious that the letter or packet would never arrive. . . . *Other letter writers wrote out and sent a duplicate letter by alternate means hoping that the success rate of delivery would be at least fifty percent* (*Paul: The Man and the Myth*, Studies on Personalities of the New Testament; ed. D. Moody Smith; Minneapolis: Fortress Press, 1999, 71, emphasis added). These facts provide a new perspective to the role of Phoebe as letter carrier of Romans.

22. D. Moo, *The Epistle to the Romans* (NICNT; ed. N. B. Stonehouse et al.; Grand Rapids: Eerdmans, 1996), 913; cf. Roetzel, *Paul*, 71.

23. E. S. Fiorenza, "Missionaries, Apostles, Co-workers: Romans 16 and the Reconstruction of Women's Early Christian History," in *Feminist Theology: A Reader* (ed. A. Loades; London: S.P.C.K., 1990), 61.

24. J. MacArthur, *The MacArthur Study Bible* (NKJV; Nashville: Word Publishing, 1997), 1723.

25. Dodd, *Problem with Paul*, 23.

26. Bauer, "ὑπηρέτην," BDAG, 1035.

27. Moo, *Epistle to Romans*, 916.

28. Dunn, *Theology of Paul*, 587.

29. V. P. Furnish, *The Moral Teaching of Paul: Selected Issues* (2d ed.; Nashville: Abingdon Press, 1985), 104.

30. Ehrman, *The New Testament*, 396; cf. Furnish, *Moral Teaching of Paul*, 103.

31. Keener enlightens us to this discussion, " 'Junia' itself is clearly a feminine name, but writers inclined to doubt that Paul could have referred to a female apostle have proposed that this is a contraction for the masculine 'Junianus.' But this contraction does not occur in our inscriptions from Rome and is by any count quite rare compared to the common feminine name; the proposal rests on the assumption that a woman could not be an apostle, rather than on any evidence inherent in the text itself" (C. S. Keener, "Man and Woman," *DPL*, 589).

32. Donalson, *Cult of Isis*, 56.

33. L. Morris, "Salvation," *DPL*, 858.

34. Morris, "Salvation," 858.

35. Morris, "Salvation," 858.

36. W. Foerster, "σῴζω, σωτηρία, σωτήρ, σωτήριος," *TDNT* 7:965.

37. Foerster, *TDNT* 7:968.

38. Bauer, "σῴζω," BDAG, 982.

39. Morris, "Salvation," 862, emphasis added. Note that "wholeness, wellness,

health, goodness" touch on *salus* being used to describe Lucius's deliverance in *Metamorphoses* as well as the nature of σωτηρία in antiquity.

40. Morris, "Salvation," 862.

41. Dunn, *Theology of Paul*, 461.

42. Morris, "Salvation," 859.

43. Of the twenty-nine occurrences, four of them are not in direct reference to salvation. Another four references are relating to humans as agents of salvation and different translations could be utilized for the same effect.

44. Bauer, BDAG, 982.

45. See NKJV, NIV, ASV.

46. "Preserved" is the translation utilized by the NASB.

47. This is the cause of much confusion regarding this verse. S. Porter observes, "1 Timothy 2.15, like few other passages in the New Testament, is almost embarrassing in the attention it draws to itself. It is one of those passages that makes discussion of 'Pauline theology,' in particular the debate over 'Paul' and women, so difficult ("What Does it Mean to be Saved by Childbirth (1 Timothy 2.15)?" *JSNT* 49, 1993), 87. Furthermore, problems concerning 1 Tim 2.15 can be pinpointed due to "a facile handling of the text, and in a failure to give due weight and consideration to its linguistic context" (Porter, "Childbirth," 88).

48. My translation.

49. Bauer, "σωτήρ," BDAG, 985.

50. Dunn, *Theology of Paul*, 329. To support this fact, papyrus letters contemporaneous with this time period have been found, where the writer inquires of the σωτηρία of others (Dunn, *Theology of Paul*, 329).

51. Bauer, "σωτηρία," BDAG, 985.

52. See Luke 4.18. However, the gospel accounts are chockful of stories of Christ healing the blind, the lame, the crippled, and so forth.

53. Bauer, "παράκλησις," BDAG, 766.

54. My translation.

55. G. R. Beasley-Murray, "Baptism," *DPL*, 60.

56. Beasley-Murray, "Baptism," *DPL*, 60.

57. Dunn, *Theology of Paul*, 447.

58. A. Schweitzer, *The Mysticism of Paul the Apostle* (trans. W. Montgomery; New York: Henry Holt and Company, 1931), 19.

59. Dunn, *Theology of Paul*, 448.

60. Dunn, *Theology of Paul*, 448.

61. Dunn, *Theology of Paul*, 446.

62. Dunn, *Theology of Paul*, 446.

63. Dunn, *Theology of Paul*, 446.

64. H. Koester, *History, Culture, and Religion of the Hellenistic Age* (Introduction to the New Testament; trans. H. Koester; Philadelphia: Fortress Press, 1984), 1:191.

65. Dunn, *Theology of Paul*, 447.

66. Emphasis added.

67. Dunn, *Theology of Paul*, 447.

68. Beasley-Murray, "Baptism," 64.

69. G. Bornkamm, *Das Ende Des Gesetzes, Paulusstudien, Gesammelte Aufsät-zen I* (München: Kaiser, 1958), 50, as cited by Beasley-Murray, "Baptism," 64.

70. L. J. Kreitzer, "Resurrection," *DPL*, 807.

71. Kreitzer, "Resurrection," *DPL*, 806.

72. Kreitzer, "Resurrection," *DPL*, 806.

73. Kreitzer, "Resurrection," *DPL*, 807-808.

74. Critical verses in this chart that are not Pauline have been designated by pa-rentheses. I understand that some of these parallels can be classified as superficial in nature, while others bear deeper resemblance.

75. Apul., *Metam.* 11.21 (Hanson, LCL).

76. While Paul's use of mystery might be dependent upon the LXX, this should not exclude the possibility of a correspondence between "mystery" in pagan religions and that as expressed in Pauline Christianity. J. B. Lightfoot is one who believes that μυστήριον is "borrowed from the ancient mysteries" (*St. Paul's Epistles to the Colossians and Philemon: A Revised Text with Introduction, Notes and Dissertations*; J. B. Lightfoot's Commentary on the Epistles of St. Paul; Peabody, Mass.: Hendrickson, 1995), 167.

77. Apul., *Metam.* 11.21.

78. These verses relate to initiation since certain individuals are selected for spe-cial roles within Pauline Christianity (i.e. apostles and prophets).

79. Apul., *Metam.* 11.25 (Hanson, LCL).

80. Apul., *Metam.* 11.15 (Hanson, LCL).

81. Apul., *Metam.* 11.9.

82. Apul., *Metam.* 11.24 (Hanson, LCL).

83. Apul., *Metam.* 11.25.

84. Apul., *Metam.* 11.25.

85. Apul., *Metam.* 11.25 (Hanson, LCL).

86. Kee, *Miracle in the Early Christian World*, 129.

87. Roeder, *Urkunden zur Religion des Alten Ägypten*, 90.

88. Budge, *Ancient Egyptian Literature*, 56.

89. Apul., *Metam.* 11.21.

90. Apul., *Metam.* 11.19.

91. Apul., *Metam.* 11.5 (Hanson, LCL).

92. Apul., *Metam.* 11.25.

93. Apul., *Metam.* 11.24.

94. Grant Showerman, "Isis," *ERE* 7:436.

95. Witt, *Isis in the Ancient World*, 22.

96. Showerman, "Isis," 7:436.

97. LiDonnici, "Women's Religions," 89.

98. Witt, *Isis in the Ancient World*, 22.

99. Showerman, "Isis," 7:436. Showerman also notes that these qualities (as mentioned above) are "to which it [the Isis cult] owed its success were the very same which existed in a fuller and less artificial form in Christianity itself" (7:436).

100. Witt, *Isis in the Ancient World*, 22.

101. Streete, "Women in Early Christian Traditions," 332.

102. LiDonnici, "Women's Religions," 89.

103. Kyme Aretalogy.

104. Kyme Aretalogy. Witt looks at the words of Gal 3.28 and compares Christ with Isis, even saying to "change *Christ* to *Isis*—and the words are still true" (*Isis in the Ancient World*, 268).

105. Kyme Aretalogy.

106. While this may be a far-fetched observation, it is a possibility that might be considered, especially in light of Isis's blatant statements of her supposed control over the sea and storms.

107. Witt, *Isis in the Ancient World*, 22.

108. Apul., *Metam.* 11.6.

109. Dunn, *Theology of Paul*, 448.

110. Apul., *Metam.* 11.1 (Hanson, LCL).

111. Apul., *Metam.* 11.7 (Hanson, LCL).

112. I am viewing the bath and the sprinkling as a combined element.

113. Apul., *Metam.* 11.23 (Hanson, LCL).

114. For instance, 1 Cor 15.35-38 is expressive in its agricultural language which might be seen to intersect with facets of the Osiris cult.

115. Keener, "Man and Woman," 583.

116. Furnish, *Moral Teaching of Paul*, 11.

117. P. H. Towner, "Household Codes," *DLNT*, 515.

118. Ehrman, *The New Testament*, 380.

119. Ehrman, *The New Testament*, 380.

120. Towner, "Household Codes," 515.

121. Donalson, *The Cult of Isis*, 19.

122. Phil 2.1-4.

123. Donalson, *Cult of Isis*, 19.

124. See Heyob, *The Cult of Isis Among Women*, 81, for more detail. S. Benko also writes of specific roles, such as the priesthood in the Isis cult in *The Virgin Goddess: Studies in the Pagan and Christian Roots of Mariology* (Studies in the History of Religions 59; ed. H. G. Kippenberg & E. T. Lawson; E. J. Brill: Leiden, 1993), 48.

Chapter Five

Isis as a
Possible Context for 1 Timothy

This chapter will focus on the religious environment in Ephesus in order to demonstrate that the Isis cult is a possible context for 1 Timothy. Evidence for the Isis cult at Ephesus preceding the time of Christ exists in numismatic, archaeological, epigraphical, and literary forms. False teaching in the book of 1 Timothy will also be explored. Finally, an examination of the Legend of Ra and Isis will demonstrate how the Isis cult can correlate with 1 Tim 2.12-14.

THE ISIS CULT IN EPHESUS

First Timothy 2.12-14 has been subjected to a variety of treatment in scholarship as W. D. Mounce has espoused in his commentary,[1] but a paucity of discussion is lacking concerning the verses addressing a specific form of false teaching. R. C. Kroeger and C. C. Kroeger offer the possibility of seeing 1 Tim 2.13-14 as "directed against Gnostic or proto-Gnostic mythology glorifying Eve" in *I Suffer Not a Woman: Rethinking 1 Timothy 2.11-15 in Light of Ancient Evidence.*[2] While this work has its flaws, particularly reading fully developed Gnosticism into the biblical text, it has made a dent in scholarship. Another contributor to the discussion is S. H. Gritz who considers the cult of Artemis as the proper backdrop for the refutation in 1 Tim 2.13 as a means to correct the "attitudes of female exultation or superiority" which is attributed to the Artemis cult.[3] However, the Isis cult can also provide a backdrop to the verses of 1 Tim 2.12-14.

While Ephesus is generally known merely as the location of the temple of Artemis, D. Knibbe seeks to correct this fallacy in his essay, "Ephesos, nicht nur die Stadt der Artemis. Die 'anderen' ephesischen Götter," for Artemis is not the only cult situated in the vicinity of Ephesus.[4] The archaeological find of this goddess has left the Isis cult shrouded in its shadows, which boasts of numismatic, archaeological, epigraphical, and literary evidence in Ephesus previous to the time of Christ.

Numismatic evidence originates from Cistophoric Ephesian coins in 88-48 BC, consisting of an Isis head decoration (literally an "Isiskopfschmuck").[5] G. Hölbl interprets these coins as accounting for the "official acknowledgment and practice of the Isis religion in Ephesus."[6]

Archaeological evidence for the Isis cult in Ephesus results from a foundation of a temple in the "Staatsmarkt in Ephesos." According to E. Fossel in "Zum Tempel auf dem Staatsmarkt in Ephesos," this cite can be identified as an "Isis-Tempel."[7] W. Alzinger and D. Knibbe also believe (in all likelihood) that this is an Isis temple (built "during the second half of the first century BC") because of the remains left there, particularly the "Glöckchen eines Sistrums."[8] Nevertheless, not all scholars, such as Hölbl, identify this temple as an Isis temple.[9] Despite discrepancies in opinion concerning the attribution of this site to Isis, one cannot escape the sistrum found here as being a telltale sign of the Isis cult. This metal instrument is used in the "ritual of the goddess"[10] and is the "principal attribute of Isis, of her priests and her priestesses."[11]

Epigraphical evidence for the Isis cult can also be found at Ephesus previous to the time of Christ. The inscription, "Σαράπ[ιδί] Ίσιδι Ἀνούβιδι Θεοῖς συννάοις" is found on an altar dating from the third century BC.[12] According to Hölbl, the only "tenable" way to see Θεοῖς συννάοις is as an appositive, resulting in the identification of the gods as Sarapis, Isis, and Anubis.[13]

Literary evidence for pre-Christian presence of the Isis cult in Ephesus has also been documented. This evidence is in a novel by Xenophon written in the third century BC called *Ephesiaca*.[14] Set in Ephesus, Isis is "cast as the preserver of the heroine's chastity."[15] *Ephesiaca* is also notable for the "geographic description *(ekphrasis)*" employed, the prominence of Ephesus highlighted, and being a survey of the "religious attitudes" of the times.[16] The importance of *Ephesiaca*, for my purposes, is that it serves "as literary propaganda for the goddess Isis."[17]

The collaboration of evidence may provide a valid license to approach 1 Tim 2.12-14 with consideration of the Isis cult. Before looking at the targeted text, it is critical to examine 1 Timothy in its larger context of the Pastoral Epistles.

FALSE TEACHING IN 1 TIMOTHY

One of the main thrusts of the Pastorals is protecting the nascent church from the danger of false teachers, whose ideas, if left unchecked, may have held the potential to permanently taint the church.[18] D. G. Horrell comments that one "distinctive feature" of the Pastorals is the "polemic against such heretics, often in the form of long strings of negative adjectives, describing those who pose a threat with their wayward teachings" as noted in 2 Tim 3.2-5.[19] Concerning 1 Timothy, the theme of false teaching resonates throughout the epistle in the opening, body, and conclusion of the letter.[20] J. A. Fitzmyer delves into more description regarding the recurrence of the false teaching throughout the epistle. He writes, "1 Timothy especially names two revilers who have swerved from the truth, Hymenaeus and Alexander (1.20); it warns against 'myths and endless genealogies' (1.4), 'godless and silly myths' (4.7), misguided asceticism (4.3), and self-appointed troublemakers (6.3-5)."[21]

The urgent nature of the situation at Ephesus can be traced to a few indicators in the epistle. The first characteristic is the absence of typical letter-writing conventions, such as a thanksgiving section (replaced by an admonition to curb false teaching) and closing greetings (substituted with a warning to avoid "τὰς βεβήλους κενοφωνίας καὶ ἀντιθέσεις τῆς ψευδωνύμου γνώσεως)."[22] The importance of the situation is stressed in 1 Tim 1.3 which is central to the epistle since it "expresses both the occasion and the purpose of 1 Timothy."[23] The subordinating conjunction καθὼς (functioning as a pro-tasis) is never completed by an apodosis in this verse. This format describes an "anacoluthon," or that which is lacking grammatical coherence.[24] The disjointed writing sequence of the author is exegetically significant for it denotes the "serious" nature of the "Ephesian problem,"[25] thereby highlighting the urgency of the situation.

The first reference to false teaching is given in 1 Tim 1.3: "As I urged you to remain in Ephesus, when I was going to Macedonia, *in order that* you may command certain people not to teach false doctrines."[26] The reference to false doctrines being taught may include those who bring Isiac myths into Christianity. Of course, this may include many more issues than Isiac ones. First Timothy 1.6 might also bear reference to the mythology used in the Isis cult. G. Fee comments on the nature of the word ἑτεροδιδασκαλεῖν (teach false doctrines), for ἑτεροδιδασκαλεῖν is "apparently coined here [1 Tim 1.3] and found subsequently only in Christian writings, literally means 'to teach other things,' or 'novelties.' "[27] Timothy is to stay in Ephesus for the purpose of preventing this strange doctrine from occurring by instructing certain people not to teach such deviant teachings. This same theme of alternate teaching is again reiterated in 1 Tim 1.4, for the author tells Timothy to instruct certain ones not "to pay attention to myths." The word utilized for myths here is "μύθοις," meaning "tale, story, legend, myth."[28] Fee writes that μύθοι in the literature of Hellenistic Judaism as well as in the Pastoral Epistles is utilized in a "pejorative sense" in order "to contrast the mythical character of many of these stories to historical truth."[29]

In 1 Tim 4.7 the author further warns Timothy that he "must reject old women's pointless myths," which may be alluded to at the end of the epistle. A literary link is established with the word βεβήλους employed in 1 Tim 6.20. Perhaps the repetition of βεβήλους serves a larger purpose—the author may be using a synecdoche to refer to the entire phrase in 1 Tim 4.7 (βεβήλους καὶ γραώδεις μύθους)—indirectly connecting the idea of old women's myths. The author's admonishment may be directed toward the Isis cult, for this popular cult appeals to women with the core of its beliefs as myths. One of these myths is the Legend of Ra and Isis.

THE LEGEND OF RA AND ISIS

The Legend of Ra and Isis may provide the cultural background for 1 Tim 2.12-14 that competes with Genesis 3. One popular feature of this legend is the role that the serpent plays in deception.

In this legend,[30] Isis, a lesser goddess, usurps the authority of the chief god (or creator god), Ra. Isis desires to know of Ra's name to become "as great and powerful" as the chief god and "thought scorn of the powers of the gods and men."[31] Ra is getting older and starts to lose control over his body, including drooling from his mouth. Isis picks up the drool that falls from the sky and couples it with the earth, forming a serpent. She fills this serpent with her magical powers and positions it to bite Ra the next day. The serpent bites Ra and he complains that "there is no pain greater than that which I now suffer."[32] Ra also has a secret name hidden inside of him so that those who work magic against him "might not obtain dominion over" him.[33] Isis comes to Ra and promises to render him pain-free if he will only give up his secret name. Ra refuses, but he does describe his works as a key to his identity. However, this is insufficient for Isis, and she promises him that if he reveals his name then she will remove the poison from him. Ra finally tells Isis, "I will allow myself to be searched through by Isis, and will let my name come out from my body and pass into her body."[34] The deceptive plan of Isis proves profitable as she learns and obtains that which she originally desired: the secret name of Ra.

Comparisons with the Genesis Account

On the onset, two of the most striking features of both accounts are the identical characters involved (man, woman, and serpent) and the act of deception. Concerning the serpent, the serpent is viewed as "a source of evil and danger" in Egyptian society.[35] This view of the serpent is a possible correlation with how the snake is viewed in the Genesis account. God curses the serpent in

Gen 3.14-15 which illustrates the evil nature of the serpent manifesting in its cunning nature and trickery. A further link between the two accounts in that the serpents are simply created beings, for the serpent should be viewed as simply one of the "animals of the earth" (Gen 1. 25, 2.19). B. Jacob writes that "Die Schlange ist nichts anderes als eben die Schlange," which dismantles ideas about the serpent being a supernatural being.[36] *gift of divination*

Just as Isis created the serpent from her magic, the etymological origin of the serpent or נחש might be related to its cognate verb form, נחש, meaning to "practise divination, divine, observe signs"[37] or the word for divination, נחש, which would inevitably foster a stronger link between the two stories. A possible connection with Ra could also be illustrated by the hieroglyphic name of Isis, meaning "seat" or "throne" (thereby demonstrating "her association with sovereignty").[38]

In both accounts, the woman, either Eve or Isis, oversteps her boundaries. First Timothy 2.12 may be reinterpreted in this fashion for not allowing Isis (or Eve) to exercise authority over a man. In the myth surrounding Isis, she exercises authority over Ra by promising to rid him of his pain, thus temporarily reversing the hierarchal structure of the gods and gaining advantage over her superior.

Later works, such as the Kyme Aretalogy and *Papyrus Oxyrhynchus XI. 1380* essentially serve as an aftermath of the legend for Isis inherits the power of Ra. For instance, Ra claims, "I made the heavens and the earth. I knitted together the mountains, and created whatever is upon it (the earth)."[39] However, Isis claims that she is the "greatest of the gods, first of names" and "rulest over the mid-air and the immeasurable" in *Papyrus Oxyrhynchus XI.1380* which pose a problem that Ra is sovereign over humanity and the gods. Isis also claims that she "divided the earth from the heaven" in the Kyme Aretalogy despite the fact that Ra claims that he "furnished the two horizons."[40] The only way to solve the contradiction between the two is to see the aftermath of the Legend of Ra and Isis emerge. Isis inherits the power of Ra as she originally desires and becomes as great and powerful as he.

Of particular note, however, is the correlation of Eve with Isis which is relevant for 1 Tim 2.13. The names of Isis and Eve further a connection between the two. The etymology of the word Eve, or חוה is notable because it correlates with חי, "alive, living."[41] Isis also has strong connections to life as reflected in Apuleius's account for she is believed to be responsible for both life and death.[42] This idea of giving life is most likely birthed in the mythology surrounding Isis for she is credited with "the revival of life in the dead Osiris."[43] Isis's role in life also extends to the idea of resurrection as noted in harvest festivals, for she is thought to resurrect the grain.[44]

Another correlation between Eve and Isis is provided in *'Abodah Zarah* 43a which reads as follows:

For it has been taught: 'R. Judah also includes the picture of a woman giving to suck and Serapis.' A woman giving to suck alludes to Eve who suckled the whole world; Serapis alludes to Joseph who became a prince [*sar*] and appeased [*hefis*] the whole world. [The picture of Serapis is only prohibited when he is represented as] holding a measure and is measuring, and that [of Isis] when she is holding a child and giving it to suck.[45]

While it may appear striking that the Rabbis referred to Isis and Serapis, it is not uncommon for the Rabbis to "refer frequently to the Egyptian deities" as seen here.[46] Concerning the goddess Isis, she is most frequently seen suckling her son, Horus.[47] Macrobius writes of Isis as covered with many breasts, which is representative of giving nourishment to all living things.[48] The goddess Eve is recorded as being "the mother of all the living"[49] in Gen 3.20 which explains how she suckles the whole world. On a similar note, the mother of all is also indicative of Isis,[50] and she is described as "*Isis lactans*," for her breasts "were said to provide the milk of life for all living creatures."[51] Isis, a goddess of "μυριώνυμος" (innumerable names), is also called "mother of the gods"[52] and is called "the beautiful animal [i.e. cow] of all the gods."[53]

The connection between Eve and Isis can also be shown in the similar nature of their temptations. The temptation for Eve is to "be like God knowing good and evil,"[54] whereas Isis is tempted to become as great and powerful as Ra. Thus, both Isis and Eve may be guilty of usurping authority over a man. While Eve challenges the authority of God's commandment, Isis challenges the authority of Ra.

The feature of pain is also a striking parallel in both accounts. Before the fall recorded in Genesis, no pain was felt. Comparatively, during his fall Ra says, "I have never suffered pain such as this before, and there is no pain greater than that which I now suffer."[55]

Another connection between the two accounts concerns the aftermath of events. In the account of Adam and Eve, God says, "See, the man has become like one from Us, knowing good and evil."[56] In the Legend of Ra and Isis, Isis learns the secret name of Ra which results in her becoming as great and powerful as he. Therefore, Eve, Adam, and Isis achieve a new level of existence.

Contrasts with the Genesis Account

Contrasts also exist between the story of Adam and Eve and the Legend of Ra and Isis. One notable difference is that in the creation account Eve succumbs to temptation and in the Legend of Ra and Isis, Ra falls into temptation.[57] This can relate to the author's words in 1 Tim 2.14 that the woman is deceived for the author may be trying to "set the record straight" for those in Ephesus and replace a myth with biblical truth.

Another difference that can be noted is that the mouth of the serpent speaks lies to Eve, which may be classified as "verbal poison." However, in the Legend of Ra and Isis, the mouth of the serpent inflicts poison into Ra. While the agent of the pain is identical, the victims in both of the accounts are different.

Based upon this evidence, the possibility exists that the author of 1 Timothy can be comparing and contrasting the creation account with the Legend of Ra and Isis in 1 Tim 2.12-14. First Timothy 2.12 can be seen as a comparison of Isis to Eve in that they both exert authority over a man. First Timothy 2.13 demonstrates that Ra and Adam are first created and not Isis or Eve.[58] Finally, 1 Tim 2.14 reaffirms the truth that the women (both Eve and Isis) are deceived, not the men (Adam and Ra).

CONCLUSION

Based upon the information of the existence of the Isis cult in Ephesus previous to Christianity and given the testimony of false teaching throughout the epistle, one can begin to approach the text of 1 Timothy in light of this historical context. Potential points of intersection of the biblical text with the Isis cult are seen in passages relating to the censure regarding myths (1 Tim 1.3-4) and the chastisement to those who are too fascinated with myths fit for old women (1 Tim 4.7).[59] A closer look at 1 Tim 2.12-14 finds the best potential for the relevance of Isis in the author's use of the Genesis fall account.

In conclusion, I have attempted to demonstrate that the Isis cult may have been a possible historical context behind 1 Tim 2.12-14. This study has differed from previous studies because it has provided a different context to assess the argument delivered in 1 Timothy, namely the Isis cult. While other pagan religions have been documented in Ephesus, particularly the notorious goddess Artemis, this is not to overlook the evidence for the Isis cult present at this vicinity. Sometimes the notoriety of a particular cult may inadvertently shroud other cults in secrecy, like the Isis cult. My goal has been to liberate the Isis cult from hiding under the shadow of other religions, such as the cult of Artemis. While it is understandable that no comparison exists between the archaeological evidence for Artemis in contrast to Isis, it is not acceptable to overlook the Isis cult in its entirety.

NOTES

1. See W. D. Mounce, *Pastoral Epistles*, WBC 46 (Nashville: Thomas Nelson, 2000, 120-43) for an overview of the treatment of these verses in scholarship.

2. R. C. Kroeger and C. C. Kroeger, *I Suffer Not a Woman: Rethinking 1 Timothy 2.11-15 in Light of Ancient Evidence* (Grand Rapids: Baker, 1992), 117.

3. S. H. Gritz, *Paul, Women Teachers, and the Mother Goddess at Ephesus: A Study of 1 Timothy 2:9-15 in Light of the Religious and Cultural Milieu of the First Century* (Lanham: University Press of America, 1991), 137.

4. See D. Knibbe, "Ephesos, nicht nur die Stadt der Artemis. Die 'anderen' ephesischen Götter," in *Studien zur Religion und Kultur Kleinasiens: Festschrift für Friedrich Karl Dörner zum 65* (EPRO 66; ed. S. Şahin et al.; Leiden: E. J. Brill, 1978), 2:489-503.

5. G. Hölbl, *Zeugnisse ägyptischer Religionsvorstellungen für Ephesus* (EPRO 75; Leiden: E.J. Brill, 1978), 27.

6. Hölbl, *Zeugnisse*, 27, cf. 20. See D. Magie's article, "Egyptian Deities in Asia Minor in Inscriptions and on Coins," *AJA* 57 (1953):163-87, for further detail regarding numismatic evidence and its surrounding implications.

7. E. Fossel, "Zum Tempel auf dem Staatsmarkt in Ephesos," JÖAI 50, 1972-75: 212-19, esp. 217.

8. W. Alzinger and D. Knibbe, *Ephesos: Ein Rundgang durch die Ruinen* (Österreichisches Archäologisches Institut; Berlin: Verlag A. F. Koska, 1972), 13.

9. See Hölbl's section, *"Die Problematik um den Tempel auf dem Staatsmarkt"* in *Zeugnisse*, 27-32, for further detail.

10. D. Magie, "Egyptian Deities in Asia Minor," 167.

11. F. Dunand, *Le culte d'Isis le bassin oriental de la Méditerranée* (EPRO 26; Leiden: E.J. Brill, 1973), 3:221.

12. J. Keil, "Denkmäler des Sarapiskultes in Ephesos," AAWW 91, 1954, 221-22; Dunand, *Le culte d'Isis*, 3:67. L. Vidman has done extensive work regarding inscriptions in the Isis and Sarapis cult. His focused comments on Ephesos can be found in *Sylloge inscriptionum religionis Isiacae et Sarapiacae* (Religionsgeschichtliche Versuche und Vorarbeiten 28; Berlin: Walter de Gruyter & Co., 1969), 153.

13. Hölbl, *Zeugnisse*, 45.

14. Donalson, *Cult of Isis*, 5.

15. Donalson, *Cult of Isis*, 5.

16. C. M. Thomas, "At Home in the City of Artemis: Religion in Ephesos in the Literary Imagination of the Roman Period" in *Ephesos: Metropolis of Asia: An Interdisciplinary Approach to its Archaeology, Religion, and Culture* (ed. H. Koester; HTS 41; Valley Forge: Trinity Press International, 1995), 81 and 82, respectively.

17. R. E. Oster, "Ephesus as a Religious Center Under the Principate," in *ANRW* 18.3:1677.

18. D. G. Horrell, *An Introduction to the Study of Paul* (ed. Steve Moyise; Continuum Biblical Studies Series; Continuum: London, 2000), 121.

19. Horrell, *Study of Paul*, 121.

20. A. J. Hultgren, "The Pastoral Epistles," in *The Cambridge Companion to St. Paul* (ed. J. D. G. Dunn; Cambridge: Cambridge University Press, 2003), 149-50.

21. J. A. Fitzmyer, "Structured Ministry of the Church," *CBQ* 66 (2004), 583.

22. See L. L. Belleville, "Teaching and Usurping Authority: 1 Timothy 2:11-15," in *Discovering Biblical Equality: Complementarity Without Hierarchy* (ed. R. W. Pierce et al.; Downers Grove: InterVarsity Press, 2004), 205-206; W. D. Mounce, *Pastoral Epistles*, 15-16. Mounce also categorizes 1 Tim 1.6-7 as denoting "historical urgency" (*Pastoral Epistles*, 15).

23. G. D. Fee, *1 and 2 Timothy, Titus* (NIBCNT 13; ed. W. W. Gasque; rev. ed.; Peabody, Mass.: Hendrickson, 1988), 7. The halting of false doctrines is also a theme that extends into Titus and 2 Timothy for it elucidates the "nature and content" of these epistles also (Fee, *1 and 2 Timothy, Titus*, 7).

24. Mounce, *Pastoral Epistles*, 16.

25. Mounce, *Pastoral Epistles*, 16.

26. My translation, emphasis added. I have highlighted the ἵνα clause here, denoting the purpose of the epistle.

27. Fee, *1 and 2 Timothy*, 40.

28. Bauer, "μῦθος," BDAG, 660.

29. Fee, *1 and 2 Timothy, Titus*, 41.

30. I have chosen to narrate the account presented by E. A. Wallis Budge, *The Dwellers of the Nile: Chapters on the Life, History, Religion and Literature of the Ancient Egyptians* (London: Religious Tract Society, 1926), 203-207. *ANET* has a similar account entitled "The God and His Unknown Name of Power," (J. B. Pritchard, ed.; 3d ed.; Princeton: Princeton University Press, 1969), 12-14.

31. Budge, *Dwellers of the Nile*, 204.

32. Budge, *Dwellers of the Nile*, 205.

33. Budge, *Dwellers of the Nile*, 205.

34. Budge, *Dwellers of the Nile*, 207.

35. Shaw and P. Nicholson, "Serpent, Snake," *DAE* (rev. ed.; New York: Henry N. Abrams, 2003), 262.

36. B. Jacob, *Das erste Buch der Tora: Genesis* (Berlin: Schocken Verlag, 1934), 102.

37. "[vx;n"],"BDB, 638.

38. J. G. Griffiths, "Isis," *The Oxford Encyclopedia of Ancient Egypt* (ed. D. B. Redford; Oxford: Oxford University Press), 2:188. However, the option as noted here "is less likely than one that alludes to a link with Osiris" (Griffiths, "Isis," 2:188).

39. Budge, *Dwellers of the Nile*, 206.

40. Budge, *Dwellers of the Nile*, 206.

41. "חַ," BDB, 311.

42. Apul., *Metam.* 11.21.

43. Griffiths, "Isis,"189.

44. Strouhal, *Life of the Ancient Egyptians*, 96.

45. '*Abod. Zar.* 43a, (trans. A. Mishcon and A. Cohen), original brackets. In determining that this statement is about Isis, Serapis, her consort when entering the Greco-Roman world, is brought into the discussion here as well. S. Lieberman reinterprets the last statement to say, "[A genuine Sarapis is] only one who holds a measure (i.e. a *modius*) and is measuring, and [a genuine Isis is] only one who is holding a child and nursing it" (i.e. Horus)" (*Hellenism in Jewish Palestine: Studies in the Literary Transmission Beliefs and Manners of Palestine in the 1 Century B.C.E.–IV Century C.E.*; Texts and Studies of the Jewish Theological Seminaries of America 18; 2d ed.; New York: Jewish Theological Seminary of America, 1962), 138, original brackets.

46. Lieberman, *Hellenism in Jewish Palestine*, 136.

47. See Griffiths, "Isis," 2:188 for a common depiction of Isis.

48. Macrob., *Sat*. 1.20.18.

49. My translation.

50. Apuleius illustrates the idea of Isis as mother in his account which describes a cow, the "fertile symbol of the divine mother of all" in the procession of the Navigium Isidis (Apul., *Metam*. 11.11; Hanson, LCL).

51. Donalson, *Cult of Isis*, 6. Apuleius also illustrates the idea of Isis as mother in his account which describes a cow, symbolizing Isis as the mother of all, in the procession of the Navigium Isidis (Apul., *Metam*. 11.11).

52. Hymn 1, line 20 of *The Four Greek Hymns of Isidorus and the Cult of Isis*, V. F. Vanderlip (American Studies in Papyrology 12; Toronto: A. M. Hakkert, 1972), 18.

53. *P. Oxy. XI. 1380* (Kraemer's brackets).

54. Gen. 3.5.

55. Budge, *Dwellers of the Nile*, 205.

56. Gen. 3.22, my translation.

57. Consideration might also be given to Ra as a portrayal of Adam.

58. In conflict to Ra as created first, Isis is described as the "mother of the universe, mistress of all the elements, and first offspring of the ages" (Apul., *Metam*. 11.5; Hanson, LCL).

59. Another possible intersection point are the references to God as Savior (1 Tim 2.3-4, 10) for Isis is thought to bestow eternal life upon her devotees.

Conclusion

The Isis cult has been examined in this work with preliminary exploration into New Testament studies. Of considerable importance is the degree of comparison between the Isis cult and the biblical text. First Timothy 2.12-14 has served as a test case to intersect the Isis cult with the biblical text. Chapter five has argued that the Isis cult may be a possible historical context behind 1 Tim 2.12-14. The Legend of Ra and Isis links with 1 Tim 2.12-14, demonstrating the Isis cult as a historical background for the author's polemic. To accomplish this study, the Isis cult has been studied from its onset through the era of the New Testament.

Chapter one examined the initial birthplace of Isis, Egypt, and the institutionalizing of the Isis cult. The origin of Isis was presented since she was one of the nine pagan deities of the Heliopolis. Ra (the father of the gods) produced Shu and Tefnut. They gave birth to Geb and Nut who produced Osiris and Isis and Set and Nephthys. Isis and Osiris fell in love in the womb and she married her brother Osiris. Because Isis was successful in this endeavor, Egyptians permitted men to marry their sisters.[1] Osiris was king, but was murdered by his brother Set in a futile attempt to seize the throne. Rather, Isis reigned over the land with complete respect for the laws and set such an exceptional example for Egyptian society that queens were given more honor than kings.[2]

This model was personified in Egyptian society by the example of Cleopatra, who was believed to be the reincarnation of Isis.[3] She exerted her power over her husband Antony (portrayed as Osiris) in terms of decisions during her reign,[4] and it was charged that he was "too much under Cleopatra's influence."[5] In terms of marital relationships, the impact of Isis affected Egyptian society, and wives took the lead in marriage relationships.[6]

An Isiac theology was also developed in the first chapter by examining the primary accounts of Plutarch, Apuleius, and Diodorus which was critical for

understanding the origin of the Isis cult. These documents were foundational
in developing a belief system concerning the goddess Isis as well as being
supplemented by the Kyme Aretalogy and *Papyrus Oxyrhynchus XI.1380*.
Drawing primarily from these sources, the powers that Isis supposedly had
were examined. These powers included everything from exerting influence in
earth and heaven as well as being a goddess of magic and healing. Attention
was also given to Isis in Egyptian culture concerning the role of women, for
she was believed to be responsible for making the power of women equal to
that of men.[7]

Chapter two discussed the assimilation of the Isis cult into the Greco-Roman world. The cult of Isis overflowed into the Greco-Roman world, and can
be placed in the context of Greco-Roman society due to the archaeological
evidence for the Isis cult in the Greco-Roman empire.[8] The Isis cult took up
residence in Rome as a permanent entity and enjoyed the endorsement of the
majority of the Roman emperors. Discussion was also given to the conflict
that the Isis cult may have presented to the Roman constitution for Rome was
founded as a patriarchal society.

Chapter three focused on Isis in the New Testament. This chapter demonstrated the Isis cult as an appropriate backdrop for the study of the New
Testament. The archaeological evidence from the Isis cult preceded that of
Christianity in many locations of Paul's missionary journeys and a striking
overlap existed between the cities in his missionary journeys and Isiac archaeological and numismatic evidence.

The Isis cult was one of the mystery religions which grew in popularity
when people became dissatisfied with the Roman state religion. Isis was a
personal goddess who would help people with their problems in life. This
was viewed as a better alternative to the Roman state religion that privileged
its own needs above those of the populace. However, the Isis cult reversed
this dichotomy by exalting the personal needs of individuals above that of
the Roman state.[9] Also, unlike the Roman state religion, Isis, the benevolent
goddess, promised to help all those who called upon her.

Chapter three also investigated Isiac beliefs and practices comparable
to Pauline practices. These included: Isis as a savior goddess, baptism in
the Isis cult, archaeological evidence for water facilities in Iseums, and a
discussion of resurrection. This study was completed by chapter four which
explored concepts in Pauline Christianity that overlapped with concepts in
the Isis cult. This chapter demonstrated that concepts existent in the Isis cult,
such as freedom, salvation, resurrection, and baptism overlapped with these
concepts in Pauline Christianity. These similar concepts may have been appealing to people within the Isis cult and Pauline Christianity because of
this common ground. The chapter developed this line of thought through
examining works of biblical scholars on freedom, salvation, resurrection,

and baptism in Pauline theology and developing comparisons and contrasts with the Isis cult.

The comparisons and contrasts with Pauline Christianity were concluded with exploring the possibility of the Isis cult as a possible context for 1 Timothy. The location of Ephesus was presented as a suitable location for the Isis cult due to numismatic, archaeological, epigraphical, and literary evidence Isiac in the location of Ephesus which preceded the time of Christ. A closer look at the contents of 1 Timothy in light of the Isis cult was also examined. Concerning 1 Tim 2.12-14, the Legend of Ra and Isis was discussed as a possible background behind 1 Tim 2.12-14.

In conclusion, I have focused on the Isis cult itself with exploratory ventures into relating this information to the New Testament, particularly 1 Timothy. I have attempted to demonstrate that the Isis cult may have been a possible historical context behind 1 Tim 2.12 -14. This study has differed from previous studies because it has provided a different context to assess the argument delivered in 1 Timothy, namely the Isis cult. While Ephesus is generally associated with the goddess Artemis, evidence for the Isis cult (including Isiac practices and beliefs) should be considered for the location of Ephesus as well. My purpose has been to highlight the historical reality of the Isis cult in Ephesus and see it as a background for 1 Timothy. With this in mind, it is appropriate to consider the biblical text as perhaps responding to or being influenced by the Isis cult, especially when considering the parallels drawn with Christianity.

This work has opened the door for further avenues of study regarding pagan religions in antiquity. This study could spawn other discussions, such as whether the Isis cult helped to pave the way for the successful launch of Christianity because people were already predisposed to the parallel concepts. If so, this could help the Isis cult gain considerable footing in New Testament studies. Despite the fact that this facet of thought has been developed by German scholars, it deserves a fresh analysis that might foster richer discussion. Further investigation into the Isis cult as a false teaching addressed in the Pastoral Epistles, particularly 1 Timothy, might also be of particular interest. It might also be advantageous to look closely at the impact of Isis in the books of Ephesians or Revelation. The Isis cult holds considerable promise for future endeavors in biblical studies and this book has untapped some of its potential in considering this historical reality as a possible background behind 1 Timothy.

NOTES

1. Diod. Sic, *Library of History*, 1.27.1.
2. Diod. Sic, *Library of History*, 1.27.2.
3. Buchan, *Augustus*, 79.

4. Hooper, *Roman Realities*, 306.
5. Hooper, *Roman Realities*, 306; cf. Buchan, *Augustus*, 102-103.
6. Diod. Sic., *Library of History*, 1.27.2.
7. *P. Oxy. XI.1380.*
8. See Witt, *Isis in the Ancient World*, 56-57, 264-65.
9. However, this is not including the prayers offered on behalf of the Roman government during the festivities of the *Navigium Isidis* as recorded in Apul., *Metam.* (11.17).

Bibliography

Abrahamsen, Valerie A. *Women and Worship at Philippi: Diana/Artemis and Other Cults in the Early Christian Era.* Portland: Astarte Shell Press, 1995.

Alzinger, Wilhelm and Dieter Knibbe. *Ephesos: Ein Rundgang durch die Ruinen.* Österreichisches Archäologisches Institut. Berlin: Verlag A. F. Koska, 1972.

Andrews, Carol. *The Ancient Egyptian Book of the Dead.* Translated by Raymond O. Faulkner. First University of Texas Press ed. Austin: University of Texas Press, 1990.

Apuleius. *Metamorphoses.* Translated by J. Arthur Hanson. 2 vols. Loeb Classical Library. Cambridge: Harvard University Press, 1989.

Bailey, Cyril. *Phases in the Religion of Ancient Rome.* Westport: Greenwood Press, 1972.

Balch, David L. *Let Wives Be Submissive: The Domestic Code in 1 Peter.* Society of Biblical Literature Monograph Series 26. Edited by James Crenshaw and Robert Tannehill. Atlanta: Scholars Press, 1981.

Barth, Karl. *The Epistle to the Romans.* Translated by Edwyn C. Hoskyns. London: Oxford University Press, 1965.

Bassler, Jouette M. *1 Timothy, 2 Timothy, Titus.* Abingdon New Testament Commentaries. Nashville: Abingdon Press, 1976.

Bauer, Walter. *A Greek-English Lexicon of the New Testament and Other Early Christian Literature.* 3d ed. Revised and edited by Frederick William Danker. Chicago: University of Chicago Press, 2000.

———. *Orthodoxy and Heresy in Earliest Christianity.* Translated by a team from the Philadelphia Seminar on Christian Origins. Edited by Robert A. Kraft and Gerhard Krodel. Philadelphia: Fortress Press, 1971.

Beasley-Murray, G. R. "Baptism." Pages 60-66 in *The Dictionary of Paul and His Letters.* Edited by Gerald F. Hawthrone, Ralph P. Martin, and Daniel G. Reid. Downers Grove: InterVarsity Press, 1993.

Belleville, Linda L. "Teaching and Usurping Authority: 1 Timothy 2:11-15." Pages 110-25 in *Discovering Biblical Equality: Complementarity Without Hierarchy.* Edited by Ronald W. Pierce et al. Downers Grove: InterVarsity Press, 2004.

Benko, Stephen. *The Virgin Goddess: Studies in the Pagan and Christian Roots of Mariology.* Studies in the History of Religions 59. Leiden: E. J. Brill, 1993.

Bergman, Jan. *Ich bin Isis: Studien zum memphitischen Hintergrund der griechischen Isisaretalogien.* Historia Religionum 3. Uppsala: Acta Universitatis Upsaliensis, 1968.

Blair, Edward B. *Abingdon Bible Handbook.* Nashville: Abingdon Press, 1973.

Bleeker, C. J. "Isis as Saviour Goddess." Pages 1-16 in *The Saviour God: Comparative Studies in the Concept of Salvation.* Edited by S. G. F. Brandon. Manchester: Manchester University Press, 1963.

Borkowski, Andrew. *Textbook on Roman Law.* Great Britain: Blackstone Press, 1994.

Bradford, Ernle. *Cleopatra.* New York: Harcourt Brace Jovanovich, 1972.

Brady, Thomas Allan. "The Reception of the Egyptian Cults by the Greeks (330-30 B.C.)." The University of Missouri Studies. *A Quarterly of Research* 10 (1935): 1-88.

Brandon, S. G. F. "Osiris." Pages 2086-88 in vol. 8 of *Man, Myth, and Magic: The Illustrated Encyclopedia of Mythology, Religion, and the Unknown.* Edited by Richard Cavendish. 12 vols. New York: Marshall Cavendish, 1985.

———. "Vegetation Spirits." Pages 2938-43 in vol. 11 of *Man, Myth, and Magic: The Illustrated Encyclopedia of Mythology, Religion, and the Unknown.* Edited by Richard Cavendish. 12 vols. New York: Marshall Cavendish, 1983.

Bremen, Riet Van. *The Limits of Participation: Women and Civic Life in the Greek East in the Hellenistic and Roman Periods.* Dutch Monographs on Ancient History and Archaeology 15. 23 vols. Edited by F. J. A. M. Meijer & H. W. Pleket. Amsterdam: J. C. Gieben, 1996.

Brown, Francis (with S. R. Driver and Charles A. Briggs). *The New Brown, Driver, Briggs, Gesenius Hebrew and English Lexicon.* Peabody, Mass.: Hendrickson, 1979.

Brown, Raymond E. *An Introduction to the New Testament.* Anchor Bible Reference Library. Edited by Daniel Noel Freedman. New York: Doubleday, 1997.

Buchan, John. *Augustus.* Cambridge: Riverside Press, 1937.

Budge, E. A. Wallis. *The Dwellers on the Nile.* London: Religious Tract Society, 1926.

———. *An Introduction to Ancient Egyptian Literature.* Mineola: Dover Publications, 1997.

Budge, Sir Wallis. *Egyptian Religion.* New York: Bell Publishing Company, 1959.

———. *Osiris and the Egyptian Resurrection.* 2 vols. London: Medici Society, 1911.

Bunson, Margaret. "Abydos." Pages 3-4 in *A Dictionary of Ancient Egypt.* Oxford: Oxford University Press, 1991.

———. "Osiris' Festivals." Page 198 in *A Dictionary of Ancient Egypt.* Oxford: Oxford University Press, 1991.

Burkert, Walter. *Ancient Mystery Cults.* Carl Newell Jackson Lectures. Cambridge: Harvard University Press, 1987.

Carson, D. A., Douglas J. Moo, and Leon Morris. *An Introduction to the New Testament.* Grand Rapids: Zondervan, 1992.

Carter, Howard. Vol. 3 of *The Tomb of Tut-Ankh-Amen: Discovered by the Late Earl of Carnarvon and Howard Carter.* New York: Cooper Square Publishers, 1963.

Cassius Dio. *Roman History.* Translated by E. Cary. 9 vols. Cambridge: Harvard University Press, 1961-69.

Cassius Dio. *The Roman History: The Reign of Augustus.* Translated by Ian Scott-Kilvert. Harmondsworth: Penguin Books, 1987.

Chamblin, J. K. "Freedom/Liberty." Pages 313-16 in *The Dictionary of Paul and His Letters.* Edited by Gerald F. Hawthrone, Ralph P. Martin, and Daniel G. Reid. Downers Grove: InterVarsity Press, 1993.

Clayton, Peter A. *Chronicles of the Pharaohs: The Reign-by-Reign Record of the Rulers and Dynasties of Ancient Egypt.* London: Thames and Hudson, 1994.

Dassow, Eva Von, ed. *The Egyptian Book of the Dead: The Book of Going Forth by Day: Being The Papyrus of Ani.* 2d ed. Translated by Raymond O. Faulkner and Ogden Goelet, Jr. San Francisco: Chronicle Books, 1998.

David, Rosalie. *Religion and Magic in Ancient Egypt.* London: Penguin Books, 2002.

"Diana." Pages 622-23 in vol.1 of *The Baker Encyclopedia of the Bible.* Edited by Walter A. Elwell. 2 vols. Grand Rapids: Baker, 1988.

Diodorus Siculus. *Library of History.* Translated by C. H. Oldfather et al. 12 vols. Loeb Classical Library. Cambridge: Harvard University Press, 1933-57.

Dionysius of Halicarnassus. *Roman Antiquities.* 7 vols. Translated by E. Cary. Loeb Classical Library. Cambridge: Harvard University, 1937-50.

Dixon-Kennedy, Mike. "Diana." Page 100 in *Encyclopedia of Greco-Roman Mythology.* Santa Barbara: ABC-CLIO, 1998.

Dodd, Brian. *The Problem with Paul.* Downers Grove: InterVarsity Press, 1996.

Donalson, Malcom Drew. *The Cult of Isis in the Roman Empire: Isis Invicta.* Studies in Classics 22. Lewiston: Edwin Mellen Press, 2003.

Donelson, L. R. *Pseudepigraphy and Ethical Argument in the Pastoral Epistles.* Hermeneutische Untersuchungen zur Theologie 22. Tübingen: J. C. R. Mohr, 1986.

Dunand, Françoise. Volume 3 of *Le culte d'Isis le bassin oriental de la Méditerranée.* Etudes préliminaires aux religions orientales dans l'empire romain 26. Leiden: E. J. Brill, 1973.

Dunn, James D. B. *Christian Liberty: A New Testament Perspective.* Grand Rapids: Eerdmans, 1993.

―――. *The Theology of Paul the Apostle.* Grand Rapids: Eerdmans, 1998.

Ehrman, Bart D. *The New Testament: A Historical Introduction to the Early Christian Writings.* 3d ed. Oxford: Oxford University Press, 2004.

"Ephesus." Pages 709-10 in vol. 1 of *The Baker Encyclopedia of the Bible.* 2 vols. Grand Rapids: Baker Book House, 1988.

Euripides. *The Iphigenia in Tauris of Euripides.* Translated by Gilbert Murray. New York: Oxford University Press, 1926.

Everts, J. M. "Conversion and Call of Paul." Pages 156-63 in *The Dictionary of Paul and His Letters.* Edited by Gerald F. Hawthrone, Ralph P. Martin, and Daniel G. Reid. Downers Grove: InterVarsity Press, 1993.

Fantham, Elaine. *Roman Literary Culture: From Cicero to Apuleius*. Baltimore: John Hopkins University Press, 1996.

Fee, Gordon D. *1 and 2 Timothy, Titus*. New International Biblical Commentary. New Testament Series 13. Edited by W. Ward Gasque. Peabody, Mass.: Hendrickson, 1988.

―――. *The First Epistle to the Corinthians*. The New International Commentary on the New Testament. Grand Rapids: Eerdmans, 1987.

Ferguson, Everett. *Backgrounds of Early Christianity*. 3d ed. Grand Rapids: Eerdmans, 2003.

―――. "Religions, Greco-Roman." Pages 1006-11 in *The Dictionary of the Later New Testament and Its Developments*. Edited by R. P. Martin and P. H. Davids. Downers Grove: InterVarsity Press, 1997.

Ferguson, John. *The Religions of the Roman Empire*. Aspects of Greek and Roman Life. Edited by H. H. Scullard. London: Thames and Hudson, 1970.

Fiorenza, Elisabeth Schüssler. "Missionaries, Apostles, Co-workers: Romans 16 and the Reconstruction of Women's Early Church History." Pages 57-71 in *Feminist Theology: A Reader*. Edited by Ann Loades. London: SPCK, 1990.

Fitzmyer, Joseph A. "*Kephalē* in 1 Corinthians 11:3." *Interpretation* 47 (1993): 52-59.

―――. *Romans: A New Translation with Introduction and Commentary*. Vol. 33 of The Anchor Bible. New York: Doubleday, 1992.

―――. "The Structured Ministry of the Church in the Pastoral Epistles." *Catholic Biblical Quarterly* 66 (2004): 582-96.

Foh, Susan T. "A Male Leadership View: The Head of the Woman is the Man." Pages 69-105 in *Women in Ministry: Four Views*. Edited by Bonnidell Clouse and Robert G. Clouse. Downers Grove: InterVarsity Press, 1989.

Foreman, Laura. *Cleopatra's Palace: In Search of a Legend*. New York: Discovery Communications, 1999.

Fossel, Elisabeth. "Zum Tempel auf dem Staatsmarkt in Ephesos." *Jahreshefte des Österreichischen archäologischen Instituts* 50 (1972-75): 212-19.

Freeman, Charles. *Egypt, Greece, and Rome: Civilizations of the Ancient Mediterranean*. New York: Oxford University Press, 1996.

Furneaux, Henry, ed. *Cornelii Taciti Annalium ab Excessu Divi Augusti Libri: The Annals of Tacitus*. Clarendon Press Series. 2 vols. Oxford: Clarendon Press, 1884-91.

Furnish, Victor Paul. *The Moral Teaching of Paul: Selected Issues*. 2d ed. Nashville: Abingdon Press, 1985.

Gardner, Jane F. *Family and Familia in Roman Law and Life*. Oxford: Clarendon Press, 1998.

―――. *Women in Roman Law and Society*. Bloomington: Indiana University Press, 1986.

Gellius, Aulus. *The Attic Nights of Aulus Gellius*. Translated by John C. Rolfe. 3 vols. Loeb Classical Library. London: Heinemann, 1978-93.

Getty, Robert John. "Isis." Pages 768-69 in *The Oxford Classical Dictionary*. 3d ed. Edited by Simon Hornblower and Andrew Spawforth. Oxford: Oxford University Press, 1999.

Grant, Frederick C., ed. *Hellenistic Religions: The Age of Syncretism.* New York: Liberal Arts Press, 1953.

Grant, Michael. *Nero.* New York: Dorset Press, 1989.

Griffiths, J. Gwyn. *The Origins of Osiris.* Münchner Ägyptologische Studien 9. Berlin: Verlag Bruno Hessling, 1966.

——. "Isis." Pages 188-91 of Vol. 2 of *The Oxford Encyclopedia of Ancient Egypt.* Edited by Donald B. Redford. 3 vols. Oxford: Oxford University Press, 2001.

Gritz, Sharon Hodgin. *Paul, Women Teachers, and the Mother Goddess at Ephesus: A Study of 1 Timothy 2:9-15 in Light of the Religious and Cultural Milieu of the First Century.* Lanham: University Press of America, 1991.

Grudem, Wayne. *The First Epistle of Peter: An Introduction and Commentary.* Tyndale New Testament Commentaries. Leicester: Inter-Varsity, 1988.

Harrison, P. N. *The Problem of the Pastoral Epistles.* Oxford: Humphrey Milford, 1921.

Hemer, C. J. "Ephesus." Pages 327-29 in *The New Bible Dictionary.* 3d edition. Edited by D. R. W. Wood, I. H. Marshall, A. R. Millard, J. I. Packer, and D. J. Wiseman. Leicester: Inter-Varsity, 1996.

Henrichs, Albert. "Dionysus." Pages 479-82 in *The Oxford Classical Dictionary.* 3d ed. Edited by Simon Hornblower and Antony Spawforth. Oxford: Oxford University Press, 1999.

Heyob, Sharon Kelly. *The Cult of Isis Among Women in The Graeco-Roman World.* Leiden: E. J. Brill, 1975.

Hölbl, Günther. *Zeugnisse ägyptischer Religionsvorstellungen für Ephesus.* Etudes préliminaires aux religions orientales dans l'empire romain 75. Leiden: E. J. Brill, 1978

Honoré, Tony. *Ulpian.* Oxford: Clarendon Press, 1982.

Hooper, Finley. *Roman Realities.* Detroit: Wayne State University Press, 1979.

Horrell, David G. *An Introduction to the Study of Paul.* Edited by Steve Moyise. Continuum Biblical Studies Series. Continuum: London, 2000.

——. Hughes-Hallett, Lucy. *Cleopatra: Histories, Dreams and Distortions.* New York: Harper & Row, 1990.

Hultgren, Arland J. "The Pastoral Epistles," in *The Cambridge Companion to St. Paul.* Edited by James D. G. Dunn. Cambridge: Cambridge University Press, 2003

Ions, Veronica. *Egyptian Mythology.* London: Hamlyn Publishing Group, 1968.

Jacob, B. *Das erste Buch der Tora: Genesis.* Berlin: Schocken Verlag, 1934.

Johns, Catherine. "Isis, not Cybele: A Bone Hairpin from London." Pages 115-18 in *Interpreting Roman London: Papers in Memory of Hugh Chapman.* Edited by Jonna Bird, Mark Hassall, and Harvey Sheldon. Oxbow Monograph 58. Oxford: Oxbow Books, 1996.

Johnson, Luke Timothy. *The First and Second Letters to Timothy: A New Translation with Introduction and Commentary.* The Anchor Bible. Vol. 35A. 1st edition. New York: Doubleday, 2001.

Jones, A. H. M. *Augustus.* Edited by M. I. Finley. New York: W. W. Norton & Company, 1970.

Jones, Alexander, ed. *The Jerusalem Bible*. Garden City: Doubleday & Company, 1966.

Jones, Allen H. *Essenes: The Elect of Israel and the Priests of Artemis*. Lanham: University Press of America, 1985.

Jordan, Michael. *Encyclopedia of Gods: Over 2,500 Deities of the World*. New York: Facts on File, 1993.

Kee, Howard Clark. *Miracle in the Early Christian World: A Study in Sociohistorical Method*. New Haven: Yale University Press, 1983.

Keil, Josef. "Denkmäler des Sarapiskultes in Ephesos." Anzeiger der Österreichischen Akademie der Wissenschaften (1954): 217-29.

Keener, C. S. "Man and Woman." Pages 583-92 in *Dictionary of Paul and His Letters*. Edited by Gerald F. Hawthorne and Ralph P. Martin. Downers Grove: InterVarsity Press, 1993.

Kittel, Gerhard, and Gerhard Friedrich, eds. *Theological Dictionary of the New Testament*. Translated by Gerhard Friedrich. 10 vols. Grand Rapids: Eerdmans, 1964-76.

Knibbe, Dieter. "Ephesos, nicht nur die Stadt der Artemis. Die 'anderen' ephesischen Götter." Pages 489-503 in vol. 2 of *Studien zur Religion und Kultur Kleinasiens: Festschrift für Friedrich Karl Dörner zum 65*. Etudes préliminaires aux religions orientales dans l'empire romain 66. 2 vols. Edited by Sencer Şahin, Elmar Schwertheim, and Jörg Wagner. Leiden: E. J. Brill, 1978.

Koester, Helmut. *History, Culture, and Religion of the Hellenistic Age*. Vol. 1 of *Introduction to the New Testament*. Translated by Helmut Koester. Philadelphia: Fortress Press, 1984.

Köstenberger, Andreas J., Thomas R. Schreiner, and H. Scott Baldwin, eds. *Women in the Church: A Fresh Analysis of 2:9–15*. Grand Rapids: Baker, 2000.

Kraemer, Ross S., ed. *Maenads, Martyrs, Matrons, Monastics: A Sourcebook on Women's Religions in the Greco-Roman World*. Philadelphia: Fortress Press, 1988.

Kravitz, Leonard and Kerry M. Olitzky, eds. Translated by Leonard Kravitz and Kerry M. Olitzky. *Pirke Avot: A Modern Commentary on Jewish Ethics*. New York: Uhac Press, 1993.

Kreitzer, L. J. "Resurrection." Pages 805-12 in *Dictionary of Paul and His Letters*. Edited by Gerald F. Hawthorne and Ralph P. Martin. Downers Grove: InterVarsity Press, 1993.

Kroeger, Richard Clark and Catherine Clark Kroeger. *I Suffer Not a Woman: Rethinking 1 Timothy 2.11–15 in Light of Ancient Evidence*. Grand Rapids: Baker, 1992.

Lefkowsitz, Mary & Maureen B. Fant. *Women's Life in Greece & Rome: A Source Book in Translation*. 2d ed. Baltimore: The Johns Hopkins University Press, 1982.

Lessing, Erich. *Ephesos: Weltstadt d. Antike*. Wien: Ueberreuter, 1978.

Lichtheim, Miriam. *The New Kingdom*. Vol. 2 of *Ancient Egyptian Literature: A Book of Readings*. Berkeley: University of California Press, 1976.

LiDonnici, Lynn R. "The Images of Artemis Ephesia and Greco-Roman World: A Reconsideration." *Harvard Theological Review* 85 (1992): 389-415.

————."Women's Religions and Religious Lives in the Greco-Roman City." Pages 80-102 in *Women and Christian Origins*. Edited by Ross Shepard Kraemer and Mary Rose D'Angelo. New York: Oxford University Press, 1999.

Lieberman, Saul. *Hellenism in Jewish Palestine: Studies in the Literary Transmission Beliefs and Manners of Palestine in the 1 Century B.C.E.–IV Century C.E.* Texts and Studies of the Jewish Theological Seminaries of America 18. 2d ed. New York: Jewish Theological Seminary of America, 1962.

Lightfoot, J. B. *St. Paul's Epistles to the Colossians and Philemon: A Revised Text with Introduction, Notes and Dissertations.* J. B. Lightfoot's Commentary on the Epistles of St. Paul. Peabody, Mass.: Hendrickson, 1995.

Livy. *History.* Translated by Evan T. Sage. 14 vols. Loeb Classical Library. Cambridge: Harvard University Press, 1936.

Lock, Walter. *A Critical and Exegetical Commentary on The Pastoral Epistles (I and II Timothy and Titus).* International Critical Commentary 39. 56 vols. Edited by S. R. Driver, A. Plummer, and C. A. Briggs. Edinburgh: T. & T. Clark, 1924.

Longenecker, Richard N., ed. *Life in the Face of Death: The Resurrection Message of the New Testament.* McMaster New Testament Studies. Grand Rapids: Eerdmans, 1998.

————. *Paul: Apostle of Liberty.* New York: Harper & Row, 1964.

MacArthur, John. *The MacArthur Study Bible.* New King James Version. Nashville: Word Publishing, 1997.

MacDonald, Margaret Y. "Rereading Paul: Early Interpreters of Paul on Women and Gender." Pages 236-53 in *Women and Christian Origins*. Edited by Ross Shepard Kraemer and Mary Rose D'Angelo. New York: Oxford University Press, 1999.

Macrobius: The Saturnalia. Translated by Percival Vaughan Davies. New York: Columbia University Press, 1969.

Magie, David. "Egyptian Deities in Asia Minor in Inscriptions and Coins." *American Journal of Archaeology* 57 (1953): 163-87.

Mahdy, Christine El. *Mummies, Myth and Magic in Ancient Egypt.* New York: Thames and Hudson, 1989.

Marshall, I. Howard in collaboration with Philip H. Towner. *A Critical and Exegetical Commentary on the Pastoral Epistles.* The International Critical Commentary. Edited by J. A. Emerton, C. E. B. Cranfield, and G. N. Stanton. Edinburgh: T&T Clark, 1999.

Martyr, Justin. *The First Apology of Justin Martyr, Addressed to the Emperor Antonius Pius.* The Ancient & Modern Library of Theological Literature. London: Griffith, n. d.

Maternus, Firmicus. *The Error of the Pagan Religions.* Ancient Christian Writers: The Works of the Fathers in Translation 37. Edited by Johannes Quasten, Walter J. Burghardt, and Thomas Comerford Lawler. Translated by Clarence A. Forbes. New York: Newman Press, 1970.

Mattingly, Harold. *The Man in the Roman Street.* New York: W. W. Norton & Company, 1966.

Mickelsen, Alvera. "An Egalitarian View: There is Neither Male nor Female in
    Christ." Pages 173-206 in *Women in Ministry: Four Views*. Edited by Bonnidell
    Clouse & Robert G. Clouse. Downers Grove: InterVarsity Press, 1989.
Moo, Douglas. "1 Timothy 2:11-15: Meaning and Significance." *Trinity Journal* 1
    (1980): 62-83.
————. *The Epistle to the Romans*. The New International Commentary on the New
    Testament. Edited by Ned B. Stonehouse, F. F. Bruce, and Gordon D. Fee. Grand
    Rapids: William B. Eerdmans, 1996.
Morris, L. "Salvation." Pates 858-62 in *Dictionary of Paul and His Letters*. Edited
    by Gerald F. Hawthorne, Ralph P. Martin, and Daniel G. Reid. Downers Grove:
    InterVarsity, 1993.
Mounce, William D. *The Analytical Lexicon to the Greek New Testament*. Grand
    Rapids: Zondervan Publishing House, 1993.
————. *Pastoral Epistles*. Word Biblical Commentary 46. Nashville: Thomas Nel-
    son, 2000.
Nagle, D. Brendan. *The Ancient World: A Social and Cultural History*. 5th ed. New
    Jersey: Prentice Hall, 2002.
Nagel, Georges. "The 'Mysteries' of Osiris in Ancient Egypt." Pages 119-34 in
    The Mysteries: Papers from the Eranos Yearbooks. Bollingen Series. 30 vols.
    Vol. 2 of *Papers from the Eranos Yearbooks*. Edited by Joseph Campbell.
    Translated by Ralph Manheim and R. F. C. Hull. Princeton: Princeton Univer-
    sity Press, 1955.
Osborne, Grant R. "Hermeneutics and Women in the Church." *Journal of the Evan-
    gelical Theological Society* 20 (1977): 337-52.
Oster, Richard E. "Ephesus." Pages 542-49 in vol. 2 of *The Anchor Bible Dictionary*.
    Edited by David Noel Freedman. 6 vols. New York: Doubleday, 1992.
————. "Ephesus as a Religious Center Under the Principate." *Aufstieg und Nieder-
    gang der römischen Welt: Geschichte und Kultur Roms im Spiegel der neueren
    Forschung* 18.3: 1661-728. Part 2, *Principat*, 18.3. Edited by H. Temporini and W.
    Haase. Berlin: Walter De Gruyter, 1972.
————. "The Ephesian Artemis as an Opponent of Early Christianity." Jahrbuch für
    Antike und Christentum (19) 1976: 27-44.
Page, T. E. & W. H. D. Rouse, eds. *The Apostolic Fathers*. 2 vols. Translated by Kir-
    sopp Lake. New York: Macmillan, 1912.
Pagels, Elaine. "Adam and Eve and the Serpent in Genesis 1-3." Pages 412-23 in *Im-
    ages of the Feminine in Gnosticism*. Edited by Karen L. King. Harrisburg: Trinity
    Press International, 1988.
Paris, Ginette. *Pagan Meditations: The Worlds of Aphrodite, Artemis, and Hestia*.
    Translated by Gwendolyn Moore. Woodstock: Spring Publications, 1986.
Pinch, Geraldine. *Magic in Ancient Egypt*. Austin: University of Texas Press, 1994.
Pliny. *Natural History*. Translated by H. Rackham. 10 vols. Loeb Classical Library.
    Cambridge: Harvard University Press, 1947-63.
Plutarch. *Moralia*. Translated by Frank Cole Babbitt, W. C. Helmbold, and Harold
    North Fowler. 14 vols. Loeb Classical Library. Cambridge: Harvard University
    Press, 1927-39.

————. *Plutarch's Lives*. Translated by Bernadotte Perrin. 11 vols. Loeb Classical Library. Cambridge: Harvard University Press, 1968-82.

Poo, Mu-Chou. *Wine and Wine Offering in the Religion of Ancient Egypt*. Studies in Egyptology. Edited by Geoffrey Thorndike Martin. London: Kegan Paul International, 1995.

Pomeroy, Sarah B. *Goddesses, Whores, Wives, and Slaves: Women in Classical Antiquity*. New York: Schocken Books, 1995.

Porter, Stanley E. *Idioms in the Greek New Testament*. 2d edition. Sheffield: Sheffield Academic Press, 1992.

————. "What Does It Mean to be Saved by Childbirth (1 Timothy 2.15)?" *Journal for the Study of the New Testament* 49 (1993): 87-102.

Powers, Eliza. *Nero*. World Leaders Past & Present. Edited by Nancy Toff. New York: Chelsea House Publishers, 1988.

Pritchard, James B, ed. *Ancient Near Eastern Texts Relating to the Old Testament*. 3d ed. Princeton: Princeton University Press, 1969.

Quirke, Stephen and Jeffrey Spencer, eds. *The British Museum Book of Ancient Egypt*. New York: Thames and Hudson, 1992.

Rahner, Hugo. "The Christian Mystery and the Pagan Mysteries." Pages 337-401 in *The Mysteries: Papers from the Eranos Yearbooks*. Bollingen Series 30. Vol. 2 of *Papers from the Eranos Yearbooks*. Edited by Joseph Campbell. Translated by Ralph Manheim and R. F. C. Hull. Princeton: Princeton University Press, 1955.

Regula, deTraci. *The Mysteries of Isis: Her Worship and Magick*. Llewellyn's World Religion and Magick Series. St. Paul: Llewellyn Publications, 1995.

Roeder, Günther. *Urkunden zur Religion des Alten Ägypten, Übersetzt und Eingeleitet*. Religiöse Stimmen der Völker. Jena: Eugen Diederichs, 1915.

Roetzel, Calvin J. *Paul: The Man and the Myth*. Studies on Personalities in the New Testament. Edited by D. Moody Smith. Minneapolis: Fortress Press, 1999.

Rogers, Guy MacLean. *The Sacred Identity of Ephesos: Foundation Myths of a Roman City*. London: Routledge, 1991.

Roullet, Anne. *The Egyptian and Egyptianizing Monuments of Imperial Rome*. Leiden: E. J. Brill, 1972.

Rouse, William Henry Denham Rouse. *Greek Votive Offerings: An Essay in the History of Greek Religions*. Cambridge: The University Press, 1902.

Rupprecht, A. A. "Slave, Slavery." Pages 881-83 in *Dictionary of Paul and His Letters*. Edited by Gerald F. Hawthorne, Ralph P. Martin, and Daniel G. Reid. Downers Grove: InterVarsity Press, 1993.

Russell, Donald Andrew Frank Moore. "Plutarch." Pages 1200-201 in *The Oxford Classical Dictionary*. 3d ed. Edited by Simon Hornblower and Andrew Spawforth. Oxford: Oxford University Press, 1999.

Sacks, Kenneth S. "Diodorus (Diodorus Siculus)." Pages 472-73 in *The Oxford Classical Dictionary*. 3d ed. Edited by Simon Hornblower and Antony Spawforth. Oxford: Oxford University Press, 1999.

Schweitzer, Albert. *The Mysticism of Paul the Apostle*. Translated by William Montgomery. New York: Henry Holt and Company, 1931.

Shaw, Ian and Paul Nicholson (in association with The British Museum). "Osiris." Pages 214-15 in *The Dictionary of Ancient Egypt*. New York: Harry N. Abrams, 1995.

————. "Osiris Bed." Page 215 in *The Dictionary of Ancient Egypt*. New York: Harry N. Abrams, 1995.

————. "Serpent, Snake." Page 262-63 in *The Dictionary of Ancient Egypt*. Revised edition. New York: Henry N. Abrams, 2003.

Shotter, David. *Augustus Caesar*. Lancaster Pamphlets. Edited by Eric J. Evans and P. D. King. London: Routledge, 1991.

Showerman, Grant. "Isis." Pages 434-37 in vol. 7 of *Encyclopaedia of Religion and Ethics*. Edited by James Hastings. 13 vols. New York: Charles Scribner's Sons, 1908-27.

Simpson, D. P. *Cassell's New Latin Dictionary*. New York: Funk & Wagnalls Company, 1960.

Sokolowski, F. "A Testimony on the Cult of Artemis of Ephesus." *Harvard Theological Review* 58 (1965): 427-31.

Solmsen, Friedrich. *Isis among the Greeks and Romans*. Martin Classical Lectures 25. Cambridge: Harvard University Press, 1979.

Sophocles. Translated by F. Storr. 2 vols. Loeb Classical Library. Cambridge: Harvard University Press, 1967-68.

Sourvinou-Inwood, Christiane. "Artemis." Pages 182-84 of *The Oxford Classical Dictionary*. 3d edition. Edited by Simon Hornblower and Anthony Spawforth. Oxford: Oxford University Press, 1999.

Spencer, Aída Besançon. *Beyond the Curse: Women Called to Ministry*. Hendrickson: N. p., 1985.

Streete, Gail Corrington, "Women as Sources of Redemption and Knowledge in Early Christian Traditions." Pages 330-54 in *Women and Christian Origins*. Edited by Ross Shepard Kraemer and Mary Rose D'Angelo. New York: Oxford University Press, 1999.

Strouhal, Eugen. *Life of the Ancient Egyptians*. Translated by Deryck Viney. Norman: University of Oklahoma Press, 1992.

Suetonius. *The Lives of the Caesars*. 2 vols. Translated by J. C. Rolfe. Loeb Classical Library. Cambridge: Harvard University Press, 1979.

Swidler, Leonard. *Women in Judaism: The Status of Women in Formative Judaism*. Metuchen: Scarecrow Press, 1976.

Tacitus. 5 vols. Translated by M. Hutton, Sir W. Peterson, C. H. Moore, and J. Jackson. Loeb Classical Library. Cambridge: Harvard University Press, 1914-37.

Takács, Saratola A. *Isis and Sarapis in the Roman World*. Religions in the Graeco-Roman World 124. Edited by R. Van Den Broek. H. J. W. Drijvers, and H. S. Versnel. Leiden: E. J. Brill, 1995.

Tertullian. *Tertullian's Treatises: Concerning Prayer, Concerning Baptism*. Series II of Translations of Christian Literature. Translated by Alexander Souter. London: Society for Promoting Christian Knowledge, 1919.

Thiselton, Anthony C. *The First Epistle to the Corinthians: A Commentary on the Greek Text*. The New International Greek Testament Commentary. Grand Rapids: Eerdmans, 2000.

Thomas, Christine M. "At Home in the City of Artemis: Religion in Ephesos in the Literary Imagination of the Roman Period." Pages 81-117 in *Ephesos: Metropolis of Asia: An Interdisciplinary Approach to its Archaeology, Religion, and Culture.* Edited by Helmut Koester. Harvard Theological Studies 41. Valley Forge: Trinity Press International, 1995.

Thomas, J. A. C. *Textbook of Roman Law.* Amsterdam: North-Holland Publishing Company, 1976.

Towner, P. H. "Household Codes." Pages 513-20 in *Dictionary of the Later New Testament and Its Developments.* Edited by Ralph P. Martin and Peter H. Davids. Downers Grove: InterVarsity Press, 1997.

———. "Households and Household Codes." Pages 417-19 in *Dictionary of Paul and His Letters.* Edited by Gerald F. Hawthorne, Ralph P. Martin, and Daniel G. Reid. Downers Grove: InterVarsity, 1993.

Tripolitis, Antonía. *Religions of the Hellenistic-Roman Age.* Grand Rapids: Eerdmans, 2002.

Turcan, Robert. *The Cults of the Roman Empire.* Translated by Antonia Nevill. Oxford: Blackwell, 1996.

Vanderlip, Vera F. *The Four Greek Hymns of Isidorus and the Cult of Isis.* American Studies in Papyrology 12. Toronto: A. M. Hakkert, 1972.

Vidman, Ladislaus. *Sylloge inscriptionum religionis Isiacae et Sarapiacae.* Religionsgeschichtliche Versuche und Vorarbeiten 28. Berlin: Walter de Gruyter & Co., 1969.

Walworth, Nancy Zinsser. *Augustus Caesar.* World Leaders Past & Present. Edited by John W. Selfridge. New York: Chelsea House Publishers, 1989.

Walters, James C. "The Coincidence of the Expansion of Christianity and the Egyptian Cults in Imperial Ephesos." Pages 315-24 in *100 Jahre Österreichische Forschungen in Ephesos: Akten des Symposions.* Edited by Barbara Brandt and Karl R. Krierer. Österreichische Akademie der Wissenschaften. Philosophicsh-Historische Klasse. 3 vols. Wein: Verlag der Österreichischen Akademie der Wissenschaften, 1999.

———. "Egyptian Religions in Ephesos." Pages 281-310 in *Ephesos: Metropolis of Asia: An Interdisciplinary Approach to its Archaeology, Religion, and Culture.* Edited by Helmut Koester. Harvard Theological Studies 41. Valley Forge: Trinity Press International, 1995.

Walton, Francis Redding and John Scheid. "Cybele." Pages 416-17 in *The Oxford Classical Dictionary.* 3d ed. Edited by Simon Hornblower and Andrew Spawforth. Oxford: Oxford University Press, 1999.

Walton, John H. *Chronological and Background Charts of the Old Testament.* Grand Rapids: Zondervan Publishing House, 1978.

Wiedemann, Alfred. *Religion of the Ancient Egyptians.* New York: G. P. Putnam's Sons, 1897.

Weigall, Arthur. *Nero: The Singing Emperor of Rome.* New York: G. P. Putnam's Sons, 1930.

Wild, Robert A. *Mystery Religions Lecture Series: The Isis-Sarapis Cult.* Vol. 6. Evanston: Religion and Ethics Institute, 1978. Slides and corresponding script.

———. *Water in the Cultic Worship of Isis and Sarapis.* Leiden: E. J. Brill, 1981.

Willloughby, Harold R. *Pagan Regeneration: A Study of Mystery Initiations in the Graeco-Roman World.* Chicago: University of Chicago Press, 1929.

Winspear, Alban Dewes and Lenore Kramp Geweke. *Augustus and the Reconstruction of Roman Government and Society.* University of Wisconsin Series in the Social Sciences and History 24. Madison: University of Wisconsin, 1935.

Witt, R. E. "Isis-Hellas." *Proceedings of the Cambridge Philological Society* 12 (1966): 48-69.

———. *Isis in the Ancient World.* Baltimore: John Hopkins University Press, 1971.

Yamauchi, Edwin. *Pre-Christian Gnosticism.* Grand Rapids: Eerdmans, 1973.

Young, Serinity, ed. *An Anthology of Sacred Texts by and about Women.* New York: Crossroad, 1994.

Author Biographical Sketch

Elizabeth A. McCabe is a doctoral student at Hebrew Union College in Cincinnati, OH. She has completed a BA in Biblical Studies from Cincinnati Bible College and holds an MA with a dual concentration in New Testament and Old Testament from Cincinnati Christian University.

Exit 5.
153 -
Broad 12th St   - 5th St
to Main   rt. → rt. → rt. Ft. Wayne
N.W. or

Little Sheba's
765.238.1990

Closeness in initiation –
"marked by a hat"

real sense of dying – pd

uth of defecation – p 30
Osiris brown pa

No power in ritual if no meaning in ordinary life.

① about writing a book like this?

What is a book that would provide an overview (systematic) of the various "religions" throughout history?

dying in mystery traditions – p. 57, p. 12

Living water – p. 60
Osiris = spring – 61
Lamentation – p. 61 – fore of the magical world

Second Temple texts 12

blood of Isis – 30

wool + wax – 18

savior – 20, 57, 76

Cleopatra 23

donkey: Set
Jesus's riding on a donkey

rebirth – 10

once nurseful – 14, 64

Osiris beds – p. 64

neither male nor female =
Paul & gender equality in Isis cult – 75

death element in mystery traditions baptism

curious describes baptism as atonement – 12